Soccer's
Most Wanted

Other Books in the *Most Wanted* Series

Soccer's Most Wanted

The Top 10 Book of Clumsy
Keepers, Clever Crosses, and
Outlandish Oddities

John Snyder

Brassey's, Inc.

WASHINGTON, D.C.

Library of Congress Cataloging-in-Publication Data

Snyder, John, 1951–
    Soccer's most wanted : the top 10 book of clumsy
keepers, clever crosses, and outlandish oddities, /
John Snyder.—1st ed.
        p.   cm.
    Includes bibliographical references and index.
    ISBN 1-57488-365-8 (alk. paper)
    1. Soccer—Miscellanea. I. Title

GV943.2 .S65 2001
796.334—dc21

                                    2001035584

Printed in Canada on acid-free
paper that meets the American National Standards
Institute Z39-48 Standard

Brassey's, Inc.
22841 Quicksilver Drive
Dulles, Virginia 20166

Designed by Pen & Palette Unlimited.

First Edition

10 9 8 7 6 5 4 3 2 1

Contents

Introduction

Soccer, the world's most popular spectator sport, originated in England during the 1850s and 1860s. The vast British empire of the era took the game around the globe during the late nineteenth and early twentieth centuries. Each country put its unique stamp on the sport. By 1930, the World Cup was established. The tournament not only decided soccer's world champion and featured the best players in the game, but it was often a fascinating clash of divergent styles of play.

Soccer rivalries, between nations or local clubs, are like none other. The most intense make U.S. college football matchups such as Alabama–Auburn, Ohio State–Michigan, Florida State–Florida, Texas–Texas A & M, or USC–UCLA look like lovefests. Soccer rivalries, many over 100 years old, take on religious, ethnic, and cultural overtones. In Glasgow, Scotland, Celtic is the favorite team of the Catholic population, while the crosstown Rangers are the favorites of the Protestants. In Buenos Aires, Argentina, the River Plate club retains the following of the wealthy side of town, while the poor and downtrodden rally behind Boca Juniors. In Spain, the two most successful clubs throughout history have been

Real Madrid and Barcelona. Real Madrid was the favorite club of former dictator Francisco Franco. Barcelona is the center of the Catalonia region of Spain. The Catalan people are an ethnic group whom Franco subjugated, often brutally, during his reign, which lasted from 1936 through 1975.

The United States has been about 100 years behind most of the rest of the world when it comes to enjoying the passions and nuances of soccer, but recently the country has started to catch up. During the 1970s, soccer began to take hold as a sport for youngsters—both male and female. At the time, the U.S. national team was a near hopeless collection of athletes with two left feet that couldn't begin to compete with the soccer powers of Europe and South America.

By the 1990s, many of those who were born during the 1970s U.S. soccer revival and had been kicking a soccer ball from the time they could walk were making an impact on the world stage. The U.S. women won the inaugural women's World Cup in 1991 and became national celebrities by repeating the feat in 1999. The U.S. hosted both the men's World Cup in 1994 and the women's event in 1999. The U.S. men qualified for all three World Cups played during the decade and reached the second round in 1994. In other tournaments and "friendlies," the U.S. defeated Brazil, Argentina, and England. The latter U.S. victory, achieved in 1993, was so shocking on the opposite side of the Atlantic that one British newspaper headline read "The End of the World." Major League Soccer began play in 1996, and the sight of Americans competing on some of Europe's top clubs is no longer a novelty.

Soccer's Most Wanted recognizes the sport's greatest victories, fantastic finishes, and champions, as well as the worst teams, outrageous characters, unlikely heroes, comebacks, injuries, outlandish stunts, odd promotions, hoaxes, unusual celebrations, curses, strange occurences, and notorious matches. The book also introduces the reader to the history and beauty of the sport, which are unfamiliar to many North Americans who know only of deaths caused by soccer riots and disasters. The world's largest and most elegant stadiums were built for soccer, and those who peruse these 60 top ten lists will begin to understand why more than 100,000 fans pack these venues on a regular basis.

In the Beginning...

Modern soccer dates from the 1860s in England, but games of football have been played in many variations all over the world for centuries.

1. CHINA

The ancient Chinese football game of *tsu chu* was first played during the reign of Emperor Huang-Ti (circa 2500 B.C.). Historians believe *tsu chu* is the earliest date ever associated with a football game of any kind. The game is known to have been used in training soldiers during the third century B.C. It appears to have been played on a regular basis in front of the emperor's palace in celebration of his birthday. A net made of silk was stretched between two 30-foot bamboo poles, and players attempted to kick a ball through a gap in the mesh. *Tsu* translates to "kicking a ball with one's feet" and *chu* refers to "a stuffed ball made of animal skin."

2. JAPAN

The Japanese played a game called *kemari,* which closely approximated soccer, as early as 600 B.C. and as late as 300 A.D. A similar game known as *kemari asobi* may have been played as late as the fifteenth century. It was connected to religious and political practices and carried out under the exacting codes of the samurai tradition. The contest involved kicking a ball through bamboo stakes clearly distinguishable as goalposts.

3. **ESKIMOS**

The game of *aqsaqtuk* was played by Eskimos in Canada and Alaska, although dates of its origin are unknown. It was contested on snow and ice by two large teams. According to one Alaskan legend, a game was played between two villages with goals 10 miles apart.

4. **ANCIENT CLASSICAL SOCIETIES**

The ancient Greeks played a game called *episkyros* resembling a combination of soccer and handball as early as the sixth century B.C. The Romans played a related contest known as *harpastum,* which was spread throughout the Roman empire. It was performed in present-day France as late as the fifth century A.D. Neither *episkyros* or *harpastum* enjoyed widespread popularity, however, as track and field and wrestling were viewed as the supreme tests of athletic prowess. An Egyptian tomb dating from 2000 B.C. depicts a man juggling a ball approximately six inches in diameter, but this endeavor doesn't appear to have been part of a team game.

5. **PRE-COLUMBIAN SOCIETIES**

Advanced football games were played in Mexico and Central America during the pre-Columbian era. Variations were played by the Aztecs, Mayans, and Zapotecs from roughly 600 A.D. until the destruction of the last pre-Columbian civilization during the sixteenth century. The contests had close ties to religion. Players were supervised by religious leaders, and ball courts and fields were usually built adjacent to the temple. In the Aztec society, losing players were often sacrificed at the altar.

6. RENAISSANCE ITALY

Forms of football were played in Renaissance Italy in Florence between the fifteenth and seventeenth centuries. The most famous contests were conducted in connection with Shrove Tuesday, celebrating the period before Lent or the beginning of spring. It was known as *giuoco del calcio fiorentino* (Florentine kickball). It was played by the aristocracy and combined elements of rugby, soccer, and American football. The "ball" was originally a decapitated head. In 1530, a game was contested by youths while the troops of Charles V were invading the city. It's still played in Florence for the benefit of tourists.

7. ENGLAND

The best established evidence of the development of English soccer dates from the Normans in 1066, though it was certainly played in some earlier form. Virtually all known accounts of football in Great Britain postdate the Norman conquest. It was played in England and Scotland on a wide scale and gave rise to sprawling, fierce contests, sometimes between cities and towns many miles apart. Because of soccer's uncontrolled, violent nature, King Edward II banned the game in 1314, but it was too popular to eradicate entirely. It was necessary for Edward's successors to issue similar edicts to try and crush the game. James I was among the first monarchs sympathetic to football and in 1618 authorized the playing of the sport on Sunday after religious services.

Charles II sanctioned football for his servants in 1681. By the eighteenth century, football games, either resembling modern-day soccer or rugby, had nearly died out.

8. AMERICAN COLONIES

The American colonies were the first overseas territory of the British empire to play football-like games. Some form of football was played in Jamestown, Virginia, in 1609, two years after the establishment of the first permanent town in the United States. The game was soon forbidden by ordinance, however, and played only sporadically over the next two centuries. The freshman and sophomore classes of Harvard initiated a football contest in 1827. The game was played annually until the faculty banned it in 1860.

9. NATIVE AMERICANS

Native Americans in New England were playing a form of football when the Pilgrims arrived in 1620. The game was called *pasuckquakkohowog* and was played on the hard sand and beaches at low tide, usually in the summer. Teams were made up of many players, who were required to leave their weapons on the sidelines. Bets were placed on the outcome of the contest. The Indians of Oklahoma played a form of football in celebration of gathering their crops.

10. THE MODERN GAME

On October 26, 1863, representatives of 14 London clubs and schools met at the Freemasons' Tavern on Great Queen Street near Lincoln Inn Field in London to establish the Football Association and to propose a uniform set of rules. The Football Association was the world's first governing body for soccer, although it took 10 years for the organization to become truly national in scope. In 1871, the Football Association Challenge was introduced as the world's first organized competition.

Her Majesty's Empire

Soccer wouldn't have become a worldwide phenomenon if it weren't for the vast British empire taking the sport around the globe during the late nineteenth and early twentieth centuries.

1. BELGIUM

Belgium was a strong nineteenth-century trading partner with Great Britain. Soccer was brought to the country around 1860 and was included in the athletic programs of English schools of Jenkins College, Harlock College, and Xaverian College. British workers in Antwerp and the industrial city of Liege played the game as early as 1865. Clubs were soon formed by Belgians who learned the game in Britain or from British residents in Belgium.

2. SPAIN

Soccer came to Spain via the Basque provinces by British mining engineers during the 1890s. The influence is still apparent in the city of Bilbao. The club team has the Anglicized name of Athletic Bilbao, and the uniforms were copied from the English team Sunderland. A symbol of Basque national pride, Athletic Bilbao has never signed a non-Basque player. British military personnel introduced the game to Madrid, Barcelona, and Valencia around 1900.

3. **AUSTRIA**

Vienna was a center of British culture and technology during the Victorian era, and soccer was the most popular recreational pastime imported by British residents. Austrians took quickly to the game, and the first officially recognized international soccer match involving two non-British teams was played between Austria and arch rival Hungary in 1902. Austria won 5–0 in Vienna behind three goals by Jan Studnicka. The sport flourished, and Austria was a major soccer power between the two World Wars.

4. **RUSSIA**

Soccer was introduced into Czarist Russia in 1887 by British brothers Clement and Harry Charnock, whose family managed the Morozov Cotton Mills in Orekhovo Zuyevo, a town about 50 miles east of Moscow. The Charnock brothers gathered together a dozen clerks from the mill to form a team, and the popularity of the sport spread quickly through the country.

5. **GERMANY**

Soccer was introduced to Germany by British residents through the North Sea ports and Berlin in 1870. In 1875, the Oxford University team toured Germany in the first overseas trip ever taken by a British team. The game was slow to develop because the German government favored individual sports such as gymnastics. Soccer was considered to be a brutal and boorish competition. As late as 1913, the sport was banned in schools in Bavaria. Adolf Hitler emphasized soccer during the 1930s as a way to display Germany's superiority, but Germany lost to Norway in the 1936 Olympics and to Switzerland in the 1938 World Cup. The Germans didn't become a world soccer power until after World War II, when the country was spilt in two. West Germany won the World Cup in 1954, 1970, and 1990 and was runner-up in 1966, 1982, and 1986.

6. **ITALY**

Italy is another country that enthusiastically embraced the game after it was introduced by the British. Soccer was first played in the northern cities of Turin, Genoa, and Milan. The British influence is still evident. Juventus of Turin plays in black-and-white striped shirts originally modeled after those of the English club Notts County. Milan and Genoa have teams with anglicized names. AC Milan, one of Italy's elite teams, was formed in 1899 as the Milan Cricket and Football Club by Englishman Alfred Edwards. The club was the realm of English sportsmen and wealthy Milanese residents.

7. **SOUTH AFRICA**

Soccer was first played in Africa by British settlers in Port Elizabeth during the 1860s and spread to the Dutch republics of Transvaal and the Orange Free State. The sport gained stature following the influx of British military personnel during and after the Boer War (1899–1902).

8. **ARGENTINA**

Argentina is the birthplace of South American soccer and was the first independent nation outside Europe to fully develop the game. Soccer was first played along the Rio de la Plata by British sailors and maritime workers in the early 1860s. In 1867, the Buenos Aires Football Club, the first of its kind in Latin America, was founded by British railroad workers. By 1880, an active league of British teams was established in Argentina. After the turn of the century, British players and officials were gradually replaced by European immigrants, mainly from Italy, who poured into Argentina by the millions.

9. URUGUAY

Soccer in Uruguay was introduced by British residents and workers during the 1870s. In 1882, an English professor at the University of Montevideo formed the first club, composed entirely of British students. In 1899, Nacional became the first native Uruguayan club.

10. BRAZIL

Soccer was brought to South America's largest country by Charles Miller, Brazilian-born son of English parents. He returned from school in Southampton, England, with two soccer balls in his luggage and organized competitions among fellow British residents at the Sao Paulo Railway Company, where he was employed. Flamengo, one of Brazil's top clubs, was founded as a British sailing club.

Soccer's Firsts

There's a first time for everything.

1. INTERNATIONAL MATCHES

Although England and Scotland are both part of the United Kingdom, the first official international match was played between them on November 30, 1872. The game ended in a 0–0 draw.

2. RADIO

The first radio broadcast of a soccer match took place on January 22, 1927, during a game between Arsenal and Sheffield United at Highbury Stadium in London.

3. TELEVISION

Soccer's first live television broadcast came during England's FA Cup final in 1938 as Preston defeated Huddersfield 1–0.

4. NIGHT GAMES

The first match played under lights was contested on October 14, 1878, from Bramall Lane in Sheffield, England, between two representative teams of the Sheffield Football Association. Floodlights, each projecting the equivalent light of 8,000 candles, were mounted on 30-foot poles, one at each corner of the field. The power was supplied by a pair of Siemens dynamo engines situated behind each goal. The use of lights for soccer matches in England didn't become widespread until the 1920s, however.

5. NOTTINGHAM FOREST

England's Nottingham Forest club was, during the 19th century, the first to introduce shin guards, the referee's whistle, the goalpost crossbar, and goal netting.

6. OLYMPICS

The first Olympic soccer competition was an unofficial exhibition held in conjunction with the first modern Olympic Games in Athens, Greece, in 1896. The match pitted a squad from Denmark against one representing Greece. The result of the match has unfortunately been lost to history.

7. SOREN LERBY

On November 13, 1985, Danish midfielder Soren Lerby became the first player to compete for two different teams in two different countries on the same day. Lerby's exhausting day began in Dublin, Ireland, as he helped Denmark to a 4–1 win in a World Cup qualifying match against Ireland. Lerby left the match in the 58th minute with Denmark leading 3–1 and took a private jet supplied by his club, Bayern Munich, to West Germany for a third-round cup game in Bachum. Lerby came in as a halftime substitute in a 1–1 draw.

8. **SOCCER AND FOOTBALL**

Soccer historians claim the first soccer match between two collegiate teams took place in 1869 between Princeton and Rutgers in New Brunswick, New Jersey. Rutgers won 6–4. College football historians trace the origins of their sport to the exact same contest.

9. **ONEIDA FOOTBALL CLUB**

The first organized soccer team in the United States was the Oneida Football Club of Boston. It was founded in 1862 and ceased operation in 1865 after three undefeated seasons in which the team didn't allow a goal. The players came from Boston high schools. Established by Gerrit Smith Miller, Oneida was also the first soccer club formed outside of England. The matches were played on Boston Common, and, in 1925, the seven surviving members of the team placed a six-foot-high monument on Boston Common in memory of the club.

10. **FEMALE REFEREES**

Referee Wendy Toms and assistants Janie Frampton and Amy Rayner became the first all-women team of officials at a men's professional match on September 13, 1999. The three officiated a minor-league match in England between the Kidderminster Harriers and Nuneaton Borough.

World Cup Firsts

The World Cup, held to determine soccer's world champions, began in 1930. It has been played every four years since, with the exception of 1942 and 1946, due to World War II and its aftermath. This list covers firsts in World Cup play.

1. FIRST MATCH

The first World Cup match took place on July 13, 1930, between France and Mexico in Montevideo, Uruguay. France won 4–1. Lucien Laurent of France scored the first goal.

2. EGYPT

The 1934 Egyptian team was the first from Africa to play in a World Cup final-round game. Egypt played only one game in the 1934 tournament and lost 4–2 to Hungary in Naples, Italy. Egypt didn't play in the final rounds again until 1990, when the country played three matches with a defeat and two ties.

3. DUTCH EAST INDIES

The Dutch East Indies (today known as Indonesia) qualified for the World Cup final round in 1938 as the first ever representative from Asia. The team made the long journey to France to play only one match, a 6–0 loss to Hungary in Reims. It is the only World Cup final-round contest in the country's history.

4. ANTONY PUSATCH

Substitutions weren't permitted in World Cup play until 1970. The first was Antony Pusatch of the Soviet Union, who was inserted into the match against Mexico on May 31, 1970, in Mexico City. The contest ended in a scoreless tie. In the Soviet Union's three subsequent matches, Pusatch was a starter in one and failed to appear in the other two.

5. JUAN BASAGUEN

Juan Basaguen of Mexico made history on June 7, 1970, against El Salvador by becoming the first substitute to replace a substitute in a World Cup final-round match and the first substitute to score a goal, helping Mexico to a 4–0 victory.

6. PEDRO CEA

Uruguay's Pedro Cea was the first player to score in an Olympic final and a World Cup final. In the 1924 Olympic gold-medal match, Cea connected in a 3–0 win over Switzerland. He also had a score in the first World Cup final, as Uruguay defeated Argentina 4–2.

7. **ENGLAND VS. BRAZIL, 1958**

Scoreless draws have become relatively commonplace in recent World Cup play, but the first one didn't occur until 1958, the sixth tournament, when England and Brazil battled 90 minutes without a goal in Gothenburg, Sweden.

8. **TELEVISION**

The first World Cup telecast occurred on June 16, 1954, when Yugoslavia defeated France 1–0 in Lausanne, Switzerland.

9. **WORLD CUP WILLIE**

The first World Cup mascot was World Cup Willie at the 1966 tournament in England. Willie was a lion-like boy.

10. **WOMEN'S WORLD CUP**

The first women's World Cup took place in 1991. In the final, the United States defeated Norway 2–1 before a capacity crowd of 65,000 at Tianhe Stadium in Guangzhou, China. With two minutes remaining in regulation, Michelle Akers-Stahl stole a weak back pass from a Norwegian defender and scored the first goal, which broke a 1–1 tie. The U.S. women were unbeaten in six matches, and Akers-Stahl scored ten goals.

The Only Time It Happened

S ome things have happened only once in World Cup play.

1. PONTIAC SILVERDOME

The Pontiac Silverdome in Pontiac, Michigan, is the only indoor stadium to be used during the World Cup final rounds. World Cup rules require grass fields, which created a problem for the Silverdome, since it had an artificial surface, and grass couldn't be grown inside. The solution? A $2.4 million field of grass was grown in the Silverdome's parking lot by agricultural experts from Michigan State University. The mixture of perennial rye and Kentucky bluegrass was then laid atop the Astroturf in 1,988 sections of sod.

2. THE NETHERLANDS

The Netherlands is the only nation to lose back-to-back World Cup finals without ever claiming a championship. The rise of Dutch soccer during the 1970s was a superb success story. The country reached the final round in 1974 for the first time since 1938. A 4–0 victory over Argentina in the first contest of the tournament was the Netherlands' first win ever in the final round competition. The Dutch made it all the way to the final before losing to West Germany 2–1. In 1978, the Netherlands reached the final again, only to be defeated 3–1 by Argentina.

3. **ITALY**

Italy is the only nation to win two World Cups and the Olympics in a four-year span. Italy won World Cup titles in both 1934 and 1938 and captured the gold medal in the 1936 Olympics in Berlin. Italy is third behind only Brazil and Germany in the all-time World Cup standings with 38 victories, 12 defeats, and 16 ties. The Italians were also champions in 1982 and runners-up in 1970 and 1994.

4. **PELE**

Acknowledged by most as the greatest soccer player in history, Pele is the only man to play on three World Cup championship teams. Born Edson Arantes do Nascimento, Pele participated in the World Cup as a member of Brazil's national team in 1958, 1962, 1966, and 1970. He gained international recognition at the 1958 World Cup in Sweden as a 17-year-old with six goals, despite his missing the first two matches due to an injury. Injuries also reduced his playing time in 1962 and 1966, as many teams went after him with brutal tackles and fouls. In 1970, Pele had his first completely healthy World Cup and scored four goals.

5. **CZECHOSLOVAKIA**

The only nation to lose two World Cup finals after scoring the first goal is Czechoslovakia. Teams that scored the first goal of a World Cup final were jinxed in the early years of the tournament, losing seven of the first ten played. It hasn't happened since 1974, however. Czechoslovakia is the only nation to score first in losing two finals, first in a 2–1 loss to Italy in 1934 and again in 1962 in a 3–1 defeat at the hands of Brazil.

6. ALDO DONELLI

Aldo "Buff" Donelli scored the only goal for the United States in the 1934 World Cup during a 7–1 loss to host Italy. Donelli was born in Naples, Italy, and moved to the United States as a child. After the 1934 World Cup, he played soccer professionally in Italy. When he returned to the States, Donelli became the only individual to coach pro and college teams simultaneously. He coached at Duquense University in 1941 and, for part of the season, was also head coach of the Pittsburgh Steelers. Duquense was undefeated in eight contests and finished the 1941 season ranked eighth in the AP poll. The Steelers were another matter, dropping all five games under Donelli's direction.

7. VAVA

Vava of Brazil is the only player to score goals in successive World Cup finals. He led his country to back-to-back World Cup championships in 1958 and 1962. In 1958, Vava scored twice in Brazil's 5–2 win over Sweden in Stockholm, and, in 1962, he scored once as the Brazilians defeated Czechoslovakia 3–1 in Chile.

8. BRAZIL AND GERMANY

The only two nations to play in more than 70 games in the final round of the World Cup are Brazil and Germany. Germany—including the years when the nation was known as West Germany—has played in 78 matches, topped only by Brazil's 80. Brazil has four championships and a record of 53-13-14. Germany has three World Cup titles and a mark of 45-16-17. Amazingly, the two soccer superpowers have never met in World Cup final-round play.

9. **YUGOSLAVIA**

The only team to have seven different players score a goal in a World Cup final-round contest is Yugoslavia. It happened on June 18, 1974, in a 9—0 rout of Zaire in West Germany. The magnificent seven were Dragan Dzajic, Ivan Surjak, Josip Karalinski, Vladimir Bogicevic, Branko Oblak, Ilja Petkovic, and Dusan Bajevic. Yugoslavia didn't use a substitute in the match.

10. **BELGIUM**

Belgium is the only nation to fail to reach the final round of the World Cup despite not allowing a goal during the qualifying matches. Only one team was slated to qualify from Europe's group three in 1974, which consisted of teams from Belgium, Norway, Iceland, and the Netherlands. Despite outscoring the opposition 12—0 in four wins and two draws, Belgium finished second to the Netherlands on goal difference. The Dutch also had four wins and two ties but outscored the opposition in group play 24—2. The two matches between Belgium and the Netherlands ended in scoreless draws.

World Champions

In the World Cup's final rounds, there were 13 teams entered in 1930, 16 in 1934, 15 in 1938, 13 in 1950, 16 from 1954 through 1978, 24 from 1982 through 1994, and 32 in 1998. There will again be 32 teams that qualify in 2002. These are the champions.

1. URUGUAY, 1930

Uruguay hosted and won the first World Cup in 1930 after capturing the gold medal in both the 1924 and 1928 Olympics. Only four European teams made the long transatlantic voyage to South America: France, Belgium, Yugoslavia, and Rumania. Uruguay defeated neighbor Argentina 4–2 in the final, played in Montevideo.

2. ITALY, 1934 AND 1938

Benito Mussolini exploited Italy's victory in the 1934 World Cup to fuel his propaganda machine. (Italy hosted the 1934 event, winning 2–1 in the finals against Czechoslovakia.) In 1938, the Italians won again in France, taking the final 4–2 against Hungary in Paris. Both of Italy's championship teams included premier players born in Argentina. These Argentinians were eligible to play on the Italian team because their parents were natives of Italy. In 1939, World War II began with Germany's attack on Poland. It would be 12 years before another World Cup could be staged.

3. URUGUAY, 1950

Uruguay chose not to defend its title in either the 1934 or 1938 World Cups but came back to win again in 1950 in Brazil. The Uruguayans were 10–1 underdogs, as Brazil was considered to be the vastly superior team and was playing at home. The first half was scoreless, but just after intermission, Friaca of Brazil scored. Uruguay's Juan Schiaffino evened matters 1–1 in the 66th minute. With 11 minutes to play, Uruguay went up 2–1 when Alcides Ghiagga drove in low near the inside post. Uruguay held on for the upset win.

4. WEST GERMANY, 1954

West Germany was barred from the 1950 World Cup, which came just five years after World War II. The Germans were given little chance in 1954, when powerful Hungary was the heavy favorite. In the final, however, West Germany shocked Hungary 3–2. It was the only international match that Hungary lost in a stretch of 48 contests between May 1950 and February 1956.

5. BRAZIL, 1958, 1962, 1970, AND 1994

Brazil fielded what most observers believe are the greatest teams ever assembled between 1958 and 1970 with such stars as Pele, Garrincha, Nilton Santos, and Carlos Alberto. During this time, Brazil logged a record streak of 13 consecutive matches without a loss (11 wins and two draws). In the

1958 final, Brazil defeated host Sweden 5–2 in Stockholm. In 1962, the clincher was a 3–1 decision over Czechoslovakia in Chile. In 1970, Brazil won all six of its matches, highlighted by three second-half goals in the final to beat Italy 4–1 in Mexico City. Brazil became the only nation to win a fourth World Cup in 1994. After 120 minutes of scoreless soccer against Italy at the Rose Bowl in Pasadena, California, the final went to a shootout for the first time. Brazil won on penalty kicks 3–2. Brazil is the only country to compete in all 14 World Cups and has a 27-1-6 record in qualifying through the 1998 tournament. The only loss came in 1993, a 2–0 decision against Bolivia played at 12,000 feet above sea level in La Paz.

6. ENGLAND, 1966

England's only world championship came in 1966 at home in Wembley Stadium. In the first final to go into extra time, England won a 4–2 thriller over West Germany.

7. WEST GERMANY, 1974 AND 1990

West Germany appeared in the final in five of the seven World Cups played between 1966 and 1990. They won in 1974 over the Netherlands 2–1 at home in Munich. In 1990 in Rome, West Germany won its third World Cup 1–0 against Argentina. Through 1998, the West Germans are 41-1-12 in qualifying. Their only defeat came in 1985 against Portugal, a 1–0 loss in Stuttgart.

8. ARGENTINA, 1978 AND 1986

Argentina won as the host country in 1978 with a 3–1 extra-time victory over the Netherlands in the final. Diego Maradona led his country to a second title in 1986 in Mexico. In the title match, Argentina defeated West Germany 3–2 with a tie-breaking goal in the 83rd minute.

9. **ITALY, 1982**

Italy went to the second round despite settling for a draw in each of its three group matches. The Italians won their third World Cup—and their first since 1938—by closing out the tournament with four straight victories. In the final in Mexico City, Italy defeated West Germany 3–1.

10. **FRANCE, 1998**

France won seven consecutive matches in the 1998 World Cup, a run which ended with a convincing 3–0 triumph over Brazil in Paris. The French had failed to qualify for the 1994 World Cup, and many dismissed the 1998 championship, believing that France won only because it was the host country. Detractors were silenced in 2000 when France won the European Cup to become the only nation in history to win the European title while world champion.

I'm Taking My Ball and Going Home

Many nations have withdrawn from the World Cup for a variety of reasons.

1. MOST OF EUROPE, 1930

Uruguay was chosen to host the first World Cup, in large part because it was the only country willing to take the financial risk involved in staging the tournament. Most of Europe, including such soccer powers as England, Scotland, Italy, Hungary, Holland, and Spain, refused to travel to South America because of the distance. At the time, there were no passenger airline flights from Europe to South America, and a journey by boat took two weeks. Counting the time to play the tournament and the return voyage, an appearance in the 1930 World Cup meant an absence from home of nearly two months for Europeans. Many professional teams wouldn't pay wages for that length of time, and amateurs couldn't afford the loss of income from their regular jobs.

2. ENGLAND, 1930, 1934, AND 1938

Even though England gave birth to modern soccer, the country (along with Scotland, Northern Ireland, and Wales) refused to compete in the first three World Cups because of a variety of disputes with the Federation Internationale de Football Association (FIFA). England finally acquiesced and played in the 1950 tournament in Brazil.

3. URUGUAY, 1934 AND 1938

Though Uruguay won the first World Cup in 1930, the team refused to defend its title in Italy in 1934 because the Italians had snubbed Uruguay's tournament four years earlier. Still angry with European nations for the snub in 1930, Uruguay also refused to travel to France in 1938, even though the French had made the trip to Uruguay in 1930.

4. ARGENTINA, 1938, 1950, AND 1954

Argentina applied to host the 1938 World Cup and, given assurances that the tournament would alternate between South America and Europe, believed it had the inside track. European teams were still reluctant to travel that far, however, and the FIFA chose France as the venue for the world championship. Miffed at the rejection, Argentina declined to compete and didn't return to world cup play until 1958.

5. AUSTRIA, 1938

Austria qualified for the 1938 World Cup, but in March the country no longer existed as an independent entity. Adolf Hitler and his army had invaded as part of the *Anschluss,* or union, with Nazi Germany. Four Austrian players were drafted onto the German team for the tournament, but the combined team lost to the Swiss.

6. INDIA, 1950

India, which had gained independence from Great Britain in 1947, looked forward to sending its own team to the World Cup in 1950 in Brazil. India withdrew, however, when the FIFA informed the players that they couldn't play barefoot, as they wished. India has yet to participate in the World Cup final round.

7. SCOTLAND, 1950

The group-one qualifying series in 1950 consisted of England, Scotland, Wales, and Northern Ireland with the top two teams advancing to Brazil. England won three matches, while Scotland finished second with two wins and a loss to the English. The proud Scots refused to participate in the final round as runners-up, however.

8. TURKEY AND FRANCE, 1950

The Turks and the French also qualified for the World Cup in Brazil in 1950 but balked when they learned of their travel itineraries in the far-flung South American country, which called for them to play matches in cities 2,000 miles apart.

9. SOVIET UNION, 1974

The Soviet Union and Chile were scheduled for a two-game qualifying playoff to determine the 16th and final spot in the 1974 World Cup final round in West Germany. After a 0–0 draw in Moscow, the Soviets refused to play in the National Stadium in Santiago on the grounds that it had been used to house political prisoners during a recent coup led by General

Augusto Pinochet Ugarte, who overthrew Marxist President Salvador Allende Gossens. The FIFA ordered the match to proceed, and Chile's eleven marched down the field without opposition and scored a "goal" at the unguarded net.

10. **LIBYA, 1994**

Libya was forced to withdraw from World Cup qualifying in 1994 because of a United Nations ban on international flights in and out of the country prompted by the threat of terrorism.

Why Are We Here?

The process of choosing the host country for the World Cup has always been fraught with complicated political intrigue and controversy.

1. **ITALY, 1934**

Italy was chosen to host the 1934 World Cup at the FIFA Congress on October 8, 1932. At the time, Italy was under the fascist rule of Benito Mussolini, who had taken power in 1922. The dictator viewed the World Cup as a great propaganda tool and wanted to ensure a spectacle that would make Italy the envy of the world. Mussolini's fanatic will to win led to some strange decisions by intimidated referees, ugly displays by crowds, and a victory for the home team.

2. **CHILE, 1962**

Chile was rocked by devastating earthquakes in May 1960 that claimed 5,000 lives, but Chilean FA president Carlos Dittborn pleaded with the FIFA to allow his country to host the World Cup. "We have nothing," he said. "This is why we must have the World Cup." The request was granted, and

Chile rebuilt its existing stadiums and erected a magnificent new one in Santiago. Sadly, Dittborn died at the age of 41 a month prior to the tournament. Chile defeated the Soviet Union in a quarterfinal match on June 10, the day Dittborn's widow gave birth to a son.

3. **MEXICO, 1970**

Athletes at the 1970 World Cup were fatigued by the intense heat, which often reached 100 degrees, and by the high altitude of some Mexican cities. To make matters worse, many matches were played at noon—when the heat was at its worst—in order to accommodate European television schedules. Fortunately, it was also the first World Cup in which substitutes were allowed.

4. **WEST GERMANY, 1974**

West Germany was selected to host both the 1972 Olympic Games, which were set for Munich, and the 1974 World Cup, with the final to be played in Munich's new Olympic Stadium. The Olympics were marred by the murder of eleven members of Israel's team, however, and the 1974 World Cup was played in a tense atmosphere under heavy security.

5. **ARGENTINA, 1978**

Two years prior to the 1978 World Cup, a military junta led by Lieutenant General Jorge Rafael Videla ousted Argentina's Isabella Peron amidst charges of corruption. The country was in a state of turmoil and an estimated 5,000 people lost their lives with many more jailed or tortured. Some European countries talked openly of boycotting the championships if they were staged in Argentina. The Videla regime guaranteed a trouble-free tournament, but new concerns arose when General Omar Actis, the president of the Argentina World Cup Organizing Committee, was assassinated by guerrillas. The tension was simultaneously elevated and eased when the *Mononeros,* a left-wing terrorist movement, announced that there would be no violence or kidnappings during the World Cup because "soccer is a game for the working class." The tournament was completed without a major incident.

6. MEXICO, 1986

Colombia was originally selected to host the 1986 World Cup but announced in 1983 that it could no longer afford to do so because of domestic economic turmoil. The FIFA wished to keep the World Cup in the Americas, and Brazil, Canada, Mexico, and the United States put in bids. Mexico was selected and became the first country to stage two World Cups, but Mexico wasn't in much better shape than Colombia. The country was going through a financial crisis and couldn't pay its foreign debts. Unemployment was a critical problem. To make matters worse, a devastating earthquake struck eight months before the World Cup, killing an estimated 25,000.

7. ITALY, 1990

In 1990, Italy cut corners in a rush to have stadiums ready in time for the competition. Safety regulations were ignored, resulting in the deaths of at least 25 construction workers. In Naples, workers drilled into what they believed was a subway tunnel and instead hit the city's main water line. The cab driver's union also nixed plans for a high-speed train line from the Rome airport to the Olympic stadium.

8. UNITED STATES, 1994

When the FIFA granted the United States the right to host the 1994 World Cup at a 1988 meeting of the organization's executive committee, there was consternation among many in the world soccer community. The U.S. had almost no soccer pedigree and had not even qualified to play in a World Cup since 1950. Hosting the tournament gave the Americans an automatic bid as one of the 24 competitors. Many observers also worried that the World Cup in the U.S. would be played in empty stadiums. FIFA believed that it was important to tap the world's greatest consumer market, not only as a source of revenue, but also to whet the American appetite for soccer. The U.S. promised to establish a soccer league in the country before 1994, a pledge that wasn't kept. Fears were alleviated somewhat when the U.S. qualified for the 1990 World Cup, though the American team lost three straight games in Italy. After the 1994 tournament drew enthusiastic sellout crowds, the U.S. was granted the right to host the women's World Cup in 1999. The United States was also placed on the front burner as a possible host for future men's World Cups, perhaps as early as 2010 or 2014.

9. SOUTH KOREA AND JAPAN, 2002

Long-time antagonists South Korea and Japan are joining forces to host the World Cup in 2002. It will be the first time that two nations have cohosted the event and also the first final held in Asia. Both countries made vigorously spirited campaigns to host the tournament, and rather than choose between them, FIFA compromised and gave the job to both. Relations between the two Asian neighbors are uneasy at best. Many Koreans openly despise the Japanese because Japan occupied and colonized the Korean peninsula for 35 years, until the end of World War II in 1945. Though many Japanese deny it, the Koreans claim thousands of women were forced to become sex slaves of the occupying military forces. When the partnership was announced on May 31, 1996, one Japanese newspaper predicted "a tinderbox of new conflicts." Officially, the competition will be known as the Korea/Japan World Cup, but when the Japanese printed the tickets in 2001, it was designated as the Japan/Korea World Cup. FIFA forced Japan to reprint the tickets.

10. **GERMANY, 2006**

South Africa was expected to become the first country on the African continent to host the World Cup but lost out to Germany in a 12–11 vote of the FIFA executive committee on July 6, 2000. Many on the committee expressed concerns about safety and instability in post-apartheid South Africa.

Gooooooooooal!

The great World Cup goal scorers include many of the top names in soccer as well as those who enjoyed one brief moment in the sun.

1. GERD MULLER

Gerd Muller of West Germany is the all-time leading goal scorer in World Cup history with 14. Known for his explosive shot and uncanny sense of positioning, Muller scored ten goals in 1970 and four more in 1974. In 1970 in Mexico, he scored three goals in successive games, first in a 3–2 triumph over Bulgaria and then during a 3–1 victory over Peru. In 1974, Muller helped West Germany win the World Cup with one goal in four different contests, including a 2–1 decision over the Netherlands in the final. Muller played three seasons at the end of his career with Fort Lauderdale in the now-defunct North American Soccer League.

2. JUSTE FONTAINE

France's Juste Fontaine scored 13 goals in 1958, the most of any player in a single World Cup tournament. Expected to be a reserve, he won a place on the squad only after an injury to Rene Biliard. Born in Marrakech, Morocco, Fontaine moved to France when he turned professional. In the third-place match, he scored four times in a 6–3 win over West Germany. He also scored three times against Paraguay in the first game of the final round, a 7–3 victory. Two years later, Fontaine's career ended when his leg was broken for the second time. Despite playing in only one tournament, Fontaine is second all-time in World Cup goal scoring. Pele is third with 12.

3. **TEOFILO CUBILLAS**

Starring for Peru, Teofilo Cubillas is the only player to score at least five goals in two different World Cup tournaments. He had five goals as a virtually unknown 20-year-old in 1970 and added five more in 1978. Cubillas may have had a shot at the all-time record of 14 goals had Peru qualified for the final round in 1974 or advanced further than the quarterfinals in 1970 or 1978. He netted his ten goals in just eight games. Cubillas was at his best on June 3, 1978, when he scored two goals and set up another in a 3–1 victory over Scotland in Cordoba, Argentina. He scored three times against Iran on June 11, 1978, as Peru won 4–1. Cubillas played five seasons in the North American Soccer League beginning in 1979 and also appeared in the 1982 World Cup but failed to score.

4. **ZBIGNIEW BONIEK**

Zbigniew Boniek was spectacular for Poland on June 28, 1982, against Belgium in Barcelona, Spain, by scoring on a pass in the fourth minute, heading a goal in the 26th, and scoring off a dribble in the 53rd. His versatility provided the only three goals of the match in Poland's 3–0 win. Boniek also played for Poland in 1978 and 1986 and had six career World Cup goals.

5. **SANDOR KOCSIS**

Nicknamed "The Man with the Golden Head" because of his ability to head the ball, Sandor Kocsis scored seven goals in consecutive matches for Hungary in the 1954 World Cup in Switzerland. Playing inside right, Kocsis scored three goals in Hungary's opening game, a 9–0 rout of South Korea on June 17. Three days later, he shot four balls into the net during an 8–3 triumph over West Germany. Kocsis scored 11 goals overall in the tournament, netting two in a 4–2 win over Brazil and two more in extra time during a 4–2 victory over Uruguay in the semifinal. Kocsis was playing in Spain in 1956 when the Soviets crushed the Hungarian uprising. He defected to the West and later played professionally in Switzerland and Spain.

6. **GARY LINEKER**

Gary Lineker of England led all goal scorers at the 1986 World Cup in Mexico by notching six of his team's seven goals. The entire English team was shut out in the first two games of the tournament, a 1–0 loss to Portugal and a scoreless draw with Morocco, but Lineker broke loose in the third contest by scoring a hat trick in a 3–0 win over Poland. He added two more as England advanced with a 3–0 decision over Paraguay, and he netted a goal against Argentina in the quarterfinals, though England lost 2–1.

7. **ERNST WILLIMOWSKI**

Ernst Willimowski of Poland is the only player to score four goals in a losing cause, and he accomplished the feat in the only World Cup match of his career. It happened on June 5, 1938, during a 6–5 defeat against Brazil in Strasbourg, France. Leonidas also scored four times for the Brazilians.

8. **PAOLO ROSSI**

Rossi put Italy into the semifinals in 1982 with three tie-breaking goals in one game during a 3–2 upset of Brazil on July 5 in Spain. The performance came out of nowhere—Rossi had been held scoreless through the first four games of the tournament. He continued his hot streak with a goal in the 2–0 win over Poland in the semifinals and the opening goal in Italy's 3–1 triumph over West Germany in the final. In 1980, Rossi had been suspended for three years for allegedly accepting a bribe and fixing a match in the Italian League. He always maintained his innocence, and the ban was reduced to two years, just in time for Rossi to compete in the World Cup.

9. **GUILLERMO STABILE**

With eight goals, Guillermo Stabile of Argentina was the leading scorer in the first World Cup in 1930. He didn't play in the first game but was inserted into the lineup for the second contest to replace a player who went back home to take a university exam. Well rested, Stabile scored three times in Argentina's 6–3 triumph over Mexico. He added two more to help beat Chile 3–1 and booted a pair in the semifinals in a 6–1 victory over the United States. Stabile scored again in the final, but Argentina lost 4–2 to Uruguay.

10. **OLEG SALENKO**

Russia's Oleg Salenko is the only player to score five goals in a World Cup match. It happened in a 6–1 win over Cameroon on June 28, 1994, turning the Indomitable Lions into meek kittens. Salenko scored in the 16th, 41st, 45th, 73rd, and 75th minutes. Despite Salenko's heroics, Russia failed to advance to the second round, and three months later he was dropped from the national team during the European Cup championships because of a series of substandard performances.

The Mouse That Roared

Nearly every World Cup features at least one team that pulls off at least one major surprise.

1. UNITED STATES, 1950

The United States pulled off what many believe to be the greatest upset in soccer history by defeating mighty England 1–0 in Belo Horizonte, Brazil, on June 29, 1950. It was the equivalent of a Division III college football team knocking off Florida State. Entering the contest, the U.S. had a record of 1-14-1 in its last 16 international matches. The team, guided by legendary Penn State coach Bill Jeffrey, took the lead in the 38th minute on a goal by Joe Gaetjens. The defeat brought banner headlines and recriminations in the English press but was virtually ignored in the United States. *The New York Times* gave it about as much space as a meaningless midsummer baseball game between the lowly St. Louis Browns and Washington Senators. The U.S. didn't qualify for the final round again until 1990 and hasn't won a final-round game in a foreign country since the 1950 shocker.

2. **COLOMBIA, 1962**

The Soviet Union figured to have little trouble with Colombia in 1962 in Arica, Chile, as Colombia had never earned a point in final-round competition. The Soviets led 3–0 after 11 minutes and 4–1 ten minutes into the second half. With one of the world's best goalkeepers in Lev Yashin, the USSR seemed assured of a win. But the Colombians struck back with three goals in ten minutes to come away with a 4–4 tie.

3. **NORTH KOREA, 1966**

The North Koreans were the only team from either Africa or Asia to enter the qualifying rounds and won a spot in the final round almost by default. To reach England, they only had to play two matches against Australia, which they won 6–1 and 3–1. North Korea was expected to be cannon fodder, and a 3–0 loss to the Soviet Union in the first match did nothing to erase that impression. The North Koreans staved off elimination against Chile with a 1–1 tie on a goal two minutes from the end of regulation. Next, North Korea produced one of the greatest upsets in World Cup history by stunning Italy 1–0. The lone goal was scored by Pak Doo Ik in the 42nd minute. It was the first time a team from Asia had won a World Cup game. In the quarterfinals, North Korea led Portugal 3–0 after 22 minutes before succumbing 5–3 as Eusebio ripped the defense for four goals.

4. **TUNISIA, 1978**

Few expected Tunisia to come close to winning a match in 1978, but the country defeated Mexico 3–1 in its first game and held defending champion West Germany to a 0–0 draw after losing a hard-fought 1–0 encounter against Poland.

5. **ALGERIA, 1982**

West Germany qualified for the World Cup in 1982 by winning all eight matches by a combined score of 33–3 and met
Algeria in the first match, a country making its first appearance in the final round. The Algerians shocked West Germany
2–1 in Gijon, Spain. Rabah Madjer scored the first goal of the
game in the 53rd minute, then set up Lakhdar Belloumi on
the second 16 minutes later to break a 1–1 tie. Algeria also
defeated Chile 3–2 but lost to Austria 2–0. Coupled with
Cameroon's three draws in 1982 and Tunisia's performance
in 1978, Algeria proved that African nations would be a force
to be reckoned with in the future.

6. **DENMARK, 1986**

The Danes didn't reach the final round of the World Cup
until 1986, then stunned everyone by winning their first
three games, defeating Scotland 1–0, Uruguay 6–1, and
West Germany 2–0 before losing 5–1 to Spain. Denmark
failed to qualify in either 1990 or 1994. In 1998, the country
reached the quarterfinals, earning two wins and a draw in
five matches.

7. **CAMEROON, 1990**

Cameroon reached the World Cup for the first time in 1982
and had three draws in three matches, including one against
eventual champion Italy. Cameroon returned in 1990 and
was scheduled to play the opening match of the tournament
against defending champ Argentina. The African nation
stunned Argentina 1–0 despite finishing the game with only
nine players. The only goal was scored by Oman Biyik in the
66th minute. In the 16-team knockout round, Cameroon

defeated Colombia before losing 3—2 in extra time to England in the quarterfinals. Cameroon became the first team from Africa to reach the quarterfinals and the first from south of the Sahara Desert to win a match.

8. BULGARIA, 1994

Bulgaria reached the final round only with a last-minute goal against France in the qualifying round. History indicated they wouldn't go far. Prior to 1994, Bulgaria had played 16 World Cup matches without a victory, losing ten with six ties while being outscored 35—11. Things didn't start well in 1994 with a 3—0 loss to Nigeria, but the Bulgarians made a surprise run with four consecutive victories, including one by penalty kicks, and landed in the semifinals, where they lost 2—1 to Italy. Hristo Stoitchkov was the star of the Bulgarian team in 1994 with six goals.

9. SAUDI ARABIA, 1994

The Saudis in 1994 became the first team from the Asian zone to reach the second round since North Korea in 1966. Many believed the Saudis couldn't score a goal, much less win a match, especially after they went through four coaches in eight months. After losing to the Netherlands 2—1, the Saudis defeated Morocco 2—1 and Belgium 1—0 before bowing 3—1 to Sweden.

10. CROATIA, 1998

The nation of Croatia, which claimed independence from Yugoslavia in 1991, competed in the World Cup for the first time in 1998. Despite political instability at home and nagging accusations that its national flag dated from a Nazi-controlled puppet state formed briefly during World War II,

Croatia reached the semifinals. The Croatians were 2−1 in group play, losing only to Argentina 1−0. In the quarterfinals, Croatia stunned Germany 3−0 before losing 2−1 to France in the semis. In the third-place game, Croatia defeated the Netherlands 2−1.

So Close, Yet So Far

I t's an accomplishment for a country to reach the World Cup final round, but somebody has to be the worst of the field.

1. BOLIVIA, 1950

One of only two landlocked countries in South America, Bolivia has been able to fight its way out of the continent's tough qualifying rounds only once since 1950, when it lost to Uruguay. Bolivia also qualified in 1930 and 1994 and has played a total of six matches in the final round, with five defeats and a draw, by a combined score of 20–1.

2. SOUTH KOREA, 1954

The first World Cup test for South Korea came in 1954 and resulted in a 9–0 loss to Hungary and a 7–0 defeat at the hands of Turkey. The South Koreans qualified for the final rounds in 1986, 1990, 1994, and 1998 and will qualify again as co-hosts in 2002, but they are still looking for their first victory. In 14 matches, South Korea has 10 losses and four draws.

3. **HAITI, 1974**

In 1974, Haitian president Jean-Claude Duvalier was so ecstatic about his national soccer team reaching the final round of the World Cup for the first time that he offered his players a $300,000 bonus for a win and a $200,000 bonus for a draw. In the first match, Haiti took a 1–0 lead over Italy on a goal by Emmanuel Sanon early in the second half, the first time the Italians had been scored upon in 13 consecutive international matches dating back to September 1972. The Haitians unraveled, however, and lost 3–1 to Italy before falling 7–0 to Poland and 4–1 to Argentina. Haiti hasn't been back to a final round since.

4. **ZAIRE, 1974**

Of all the teams to qualify for the World Cup, Zaire stands last alphabetically and finished last in West Germany in 1974 in the country's only trip to a final round. The African nation lost three times without scoring a goal while allowing 14 into the net. In its second-round match against Yugoslavia, Zaire trailed 6–0 at halftime and lost 9–0. Zaire's President Mobutu Sese Seko promised each player on the squad a house, a car, and a free vacation as a reward for qualifying, then sent them off to West Germany with the admonition "Win or die." The players lives were spared, but the offer of free gifts was withdrawn. Despite the embarrassment, Zaire can derive a sense of accomplishment from becoming the first black-majority nation and the first African country from south of the Sahara Desert to reach the final round.

5. **MEXICO, 1978**

A big fish in the little pond of the CONCACAF (North America, Central America, and the Caribbean) region, Mexico has qualified for 11 of the 14 World Cups with little to show for it. The 1978 team lost three times by a combined score of 12–2. The 19 defeats by the Mexican team is the all-time record in World Cup play. They have won eight times and have achieved 10 draws. Two of the 10 draws resulted in defeats in penalty-kick shoot-outs, which count as draws in the official World Cup standings. The record of the Mexicans has been helped greatly by hosting the tournament in 1970 and 1986. On foreign soil, Mexico's won-lost-tied record is 3-19-5.

6. **NEW ZEALAND, 1982**

It's rare for a team from Oceania to reach the World Cup. The region consists of Australia, New Zealand, and the South Pacific nations such as Tahiti and Fiji. The winner of the region in qualifying also has to win a home-and-home play-off against another team from another region to reach the final round. Only Australia in 1974 and New Zealand in 1982 have made it. Australia had two losses and a draw and failed to score a goal. New Zealand lost three times and was outscored 12–2.

7. **EL SALVADOR, 1982**

El Salvador is the only country to allow at least 10 goals in the final rounds of the World Cup, suffering a 10–1 thrashing at the hands of Hungary in 1982 in Spain. El Salvador's goal in that game is the only one the team has scored in final-round competition. The Central American country also qualified in 1970 and has a World Cup record of six losses in six matches while being outscored 22–1.

8. **UNITED ARAB EMIRATES, 1990**

The United Arab Emirates reached the World Cup for the only time in the nation's history in 1990 but appeared disorganized and confused. The team lost three times, 2–0 to Colombia, 5–1 to West Germany in a torrential downpour, and 4–1 against Yugoslavia.

9. **GREECE, 1994**

Greece reached the final round of the World Cup for the first time in 1994, but the joy was short-lived. Greece lost 4–0 to Argentina in Foxboro, Massachusetts, 4–0 to Bulgaria in Chicago, and 2–0 against Nigeria in Dallas.

10. **JAPAN, 1998**

Japan has an automatic entry into the 2002 World Cup as cohost but didn't make much of an impression in its first World Cup appearance in 1998. The Japanese lost all three matches to Argentina (1–0), Croatia (1–0), and Jamaica (2–1).

Great Moments in U.S. Soccer History

The shocking upset of England in the 1950 World Cup hasn't been the only great moment during the history of U.S. soccer.

1. **1930 WORLD CUP**

The United States appeared in the very first World Cup and won its first two matches. With a team made up largely of immigrants from England and Scotland, the U.S. defeated Belgium 3–0 on July 13 at Central Park Stadium in Montevideo, Uruguay, and downed Paraguay four days later by the same score in the same stadium before a crowd of only 800. The bubble burst with a 6–1 loss to Argentina on July 26.

2. **1990 WORLD CUP QUALIFYING**

The United States qualified for the World Cup final round for the first time since 1950 with a 1–0 road win over Trinidad and Tobago on November 19, 1989. The U.S. needed a victory to advance but hadn't scored in 208 minutes entering the match. The game-winner came on Paul Caliguri's left-footed volley from 30 yards in the 31st minute.

3. **1991 GOLD CUP**

The U.S. won the Gold Cup, signifying the championship of North and Central America and the Caribbean, in 1991. The championship match was played on July 7 against Honduras in Los Angeles. After 120 minutes of scoreless play, the title was decided in a penalty shoot-out. The U.S. won the round 4–3 with Fernando Clavijo providing the decisive goal.

4. **1991 WOMEN'S WORLD CUP**

The United States won the very first Women's World Cup, played in 1991 in China. Coached by Anson Dorrance of the University of North Carolina, the U.S. team won six consecutive matches by a combined score of 25–5. After a 5–2 win over Germany in the semifinals, the U.S. defeated Norway 2–1 in the championship match.

5. **ENGLAND, 1993**

The U.S. defeated England for the first time since 1950 with a 2–0 decision at Foxboro, Massachusetts, on June 9, 1993. The goals were scored by Thomas Dooley and Alexi Lalas. Tony Meola starred in goal.

6. **WORLD CUP, 1994**

The U.S. won its first World Cup final-round match in 44 years with a 2–1 victory over Colombia on June 22, 1994, at the Rose Bowl in Pasadena, California. After a draw with Switzerland, the U.S. reached the second round but lost 1–0 to Brazil.

7. **COPA AMERICA, 1995**

At the Copa America in 1995 in Uruguay, the United States defeated Chile 2–1 for its first win in South America since

1950. In the next match, the U.S. achieved its first-ever win over heavily favored Argentina by a 3−0 count to reach the quarterfinals. After beating Mexico on penalty kicks, the U.S. lost in the semifinals 1−0 against Brazil.

8. **BRAZIL, 1998**

The U.S. men's team defeated Brazil for the first time ever on February 10, 1998, by a 1−0 score at the Los Angeles Coliseum. Brazilian striker Romario declared that Kasey Keller put in "the greatest performance I have ever seen in a goalkeeper."

9. **DC UNITED, 1998**

DC United became the first U.S. team to win the CONCACAF Champion's Cup, which brings together the strongest teams in the region. The victory came on August 16, 1998, with a 1−0 win over Mexican title holder Toluca. Eddie Pope scored the lone goal. Four months later, on December 5, DC United became the first ever U.S. club to win the Interamerican Cup with a 2−0 win over Brazil's Vasco da Gama in Fort Lauderdale.

10. **WOMEN'S WORLD CUP, 1999**

The U.S. women won the 1999 World Cup at the Rose Bowl on penalty kicks against China before 90,185 spectators, the largest crowd in world history to see a women's sporting event. The team, coached by Tony DiCicco, touched a national nerve. In the U.S., the final was witnessed by 40 million, a larger audience than for any game in the 1999 NBA finals.

Stalwart defender Eddie Pope, *front,* scored the lone goal that led
D.C. United to victory over Mexico's Toluca by a score of 1–0 in the
1998 CONCACAF Champion's Cup. D.C. United's victory marked
the first time that a U.S. club won this prestigious tournament.

Tab Ramos, pictured here playing for the New York/New Jersey Metrostars, was a fixture on the U.S. National Team during the 1990s and a key player for the team that advanced to the second round of the 1994 World Cup.

Mia Hamm is the most prolific goal scorer, woman or man, in the history of the sport. She is also the most recognizable women's soccer player in the world.

Tiffeny Milbrett, shown playing for the New York Power of the Women's United Soccer Association (WUSA), scored the winning goal for the United States in the gold medal match of the 1996 Olympic Games.

Carla Overbeck, *left,* the captain and iron woman of the U.S. Women's team, played in every minute of every match in the 1999 World Cup. She is pictured here playing for the Carolina Courage of the WUSA.

U.S. World Champions

The 1991 U.S. women's world champions played in almost complete obscurity. The 1999 winners became national celebrities overnight.

1. MIA HAMM

When she scored her 108th international goal in 1999, Mia Hamm set the record for the most goals in soccer history by a man or woman. Growing up in a military family, Mia moved all over the country. She picked up soccer as a youngster from an adopted Thai-American brother. She suited up for the national team at the age of 15 and played at the powerhouse University of North Carolina.

2. TIFFENY MILBRETT

Only 5'2", Tiffeny Milbrett scored the gold-medal goal in the 1996 Olympics and played two years professionally in Japan.

3. BRIANA SCURRY

Goalkeeper Briana Scurry moved from Galveston, Texas, to the Minneapolis area when she was a baby after her home was destroyed in a hurricane. Briana grew up in suburban Dayton as part of the only African-American family in a four-mile radius and began playing soccer at the age of nine.

4. BRANDI CHASTAIN

The most versatile player on the U.S. team, Brandi Chastain is best-known for her shirt-waving celebration after scoring the match-winning penalty kick against China. She was almost left off the list of five players to take the kicks, but coach Tony DiCicco had a hunch and added her at the last minute. During the 3–2 win over Germany in the quarterfinal of the 1999 World Cup, Chastain kicked the ball into her own net but redeemed herself with a goal to tie the match 2–2.

5. KRISTINE LILLY

In 2000, Kristine Lilly became the first woman ever to play in 200 international matches. Earlier, she had teamed with Mia Hamm at North Carolina.

6. JULIE FOUDY

Attacking midfielder Julie Foudy became well-known before the 1999 women's World Cup by serving as an ESPN and ABC studio analyst during the 1998 men's World Cup. She was admitted to the medical school at Stanford University but gave up her ambitions as a physician to pursue a career in soccer.

7. SHANNON MACMILLAN

From Escondido, California, Shannon MacMillan scored three goals in the 1996 Olympics, including one in overtime to defeat Norway 1–0 in the semifinals. She played at the University of Portland with Tiffeny Milbrett.

8. **MICHELLE AKERS**

Michelle Akers scored ten goals in the 1991 World Cup and, at 33, was the oldest member of the 1999 squad despite suffering from chronic fatigue syndrome. During the postgame celebrations, she was flat on her back strapped to an IV.

9. **CARLA OVERBECK**

The captain of the 1999 team and a defensive stalwart, Carla Overbeck played every minute of every match. She overcame a battle with Graves disease during the spring of 2000 to play in the Olympics in Sydney, Australia.

10. **CINDY PARLOW**

A native of Memphis, Cindy Parlow was the youngest (21) and tallest (5′ 11″) member of the 1999 team. Part of the new wave of U.S. players who were born after the soccer boom began during the early 1970s, Cindy said that she "started walking with a soccer ball at [her] feet."

Not-So-Great Moments in U.S. Soccer History

S ome moments the U.S. would rather forget.

1. **1934 WORLD CUP**

The 1934 World Cup was a 16-team single-elimination tournament. The U.S. traveled all the way to Rome only to be thrashed by Italy 7–1.

2. **1949 WORLD CUP QUALIFYING**

On September 4, 1949, in a World Cup qualifying match against Mexico in Mexico City, the U.S. lost 6–0, its twelfth consecutive international defeat dating back to 1934, including an 11–0 loss to Norway in 1948. Fortunately, two of the three teams in the CONCACAF group qualified for a berth in the 1950 World Cup in Brazil, and the U.S. beat lowly Cuba 5–2 for a spot in the tournament.

3. **1957 WORLD CUP QUALIFYING**

The U.S. played four qualifying matches against Mexico and
Canada and lost each of them by a combined score of 21–5.
Mexico embarrassed the Americans 7–2 in Los Angeles.

4. **SOUTH AMERICA, 1963**

The U.S. team took a goodwill trip to Sao Paulo, Brazil, in
1963 and played like lambs against their South American
hosts, losing 10–2 to Chile, 8–1 to Argentina, 10–0 to Brazil,
and 2–0 to Uruguay.

5. **1964 OLYMPIC GAMES QUALIFYING**

On March 16, 1964, the U.S. lost to tiny Surinam 1–0 in
Mexico City.

6. **DANNY BLANCHFLOWER**

The North American Soccer League debuted in 1967 with a
television contract from CBS. The network hired Jack Whitaker
as play-by-play announcer and former Irish soccer star Danny
Blanchflower as commentator. The league needed someone
to promote the new product in the U.S., but Blanchflower
spent the entire season complaining about the lack of talent
on the field.

7. **1973 WORLD CUP QUALIFYING**

Once more, the U.S. failed to win a match, with three losses
and one draw against Canada and Mexico.

8. **EUROPE, 1975**

A two-match trip to Europe in 1975 resulted in a 7–0 defeat
against Poland in Poznan and a 10–0 drubbing from Italy in
Rome.

9. **1990 WORLD CUP**

The U.S. reached the final round of the World Cup for the first time since 1950, and coach Bob Gansler boasted that his club was good enough to win the championship. His prediction fell a tad short, as the U.S. lost 5–1 to Czechoslovakia, 1–0 to host Italy, and 2–1 to Austria.

10. **1998 WORLD CUP**

The success of 1994 raised hopes when the national team traveled to France in 1998, but those hopes were dashed as the U.S. was arguably the worst of the 32 squads in the field. The Americans lost 2–0 to Germany, 2–1 in a politically charged match against Iran, and 1–0 versus Yugoslavia.

not Our Game

Maybe baseball is to blame for the lack of U.S. success in soccer. As a general rule, baseball-playing nations have fared poorly in international soccer.

1. UNITED STATES

The country that developed baseball and boasts a "World Series" that has had only one representative outside the U.S. in the event's 98-year history has only four World Cup final-round victories to its credit. Two came in 1930 in a depleted field, one a fluke in 1950, and another as host in 1994.

2. CUBA

Before becoming dictator of Cuba, Fidel Castro was scouted by the New York Giants, not Manchester United. The Cubans haven't reached the final round of the World Cup since 1938, when they were walloped by Sweden 8–0.

3. DOMINICAN REPUBLIC

The Dominican Republic has provided the majors with a steady stream of talent, but the country's soccer talent is almost nonexistent. Meanwhile, much smaller Caribbean nations such as Jamaica, Haiti, and Trinidad and Tobago—where baseball fields are almost as rare as snowstorms—have been tough opponents in World Cup qualifying in the CONCACAF region and have occasionally sneaked into the final round.

4. PANAMA

The birthplace of Rod Carew, Panama has delivered several players to major-league baseball, but its national soccer teams have been pushovers.

5. NICARAGUA

Like Panama, Nicaragua has no soccer tradition whatsoever. Costa Rica, located to the north of Panama and to the south of Nicaragua, has no baseball tradition but a passionate soccer following. The Costa Ricans have given the U.S. all it can handle during World Cup qualifying matches in recent years. The Central American nations of Honduras and Guatemala are likewise soccer-playing nations where a drawing of a baseball might as well be posted on signs with a red slash through it.

6. MEXICO

Although the U.S. is improving, Mexico is just about the only nation with any kind of success in both baseball and soccer. Though Mexico dominates CONCACAF, real international success for the Mexicans is still a dream.

7. VENEZUELA

To say that Venezuela is to South American soccer what the Los Angeles Clippers are to the NBA would be an insult to the Clippers. Of the 10 nations in South America, Venezuela is routinely at the bottom. An international victory is rare, and the country has never come close to reaching the World Cup final round even though four or five of the ten countries on the continent qualify for the tournament. However, Venezuela has given baseball some of its greatest stars, including Hall of Famer Luis Aparicio.

8. **JAPAN**

Soccer is beginning to make some inroads in Japan. A professional league began in 1993, and the country will cohost the 2002 World Cup with Korea. The sport won't come close to eclipsing baseball's popularity in the foreseeable future, however. Soccer may not even eclipse sumo wrestling.

9. **AUSTRALIA**

The Australians have begun delivering players to the majors during the last 15 years. The country qualified for the World Cup final round only in 1974 and failed to score a goal in three matches.

10. **TAIWAN**

Military commitments have prevented Taiwan's top baseball players from playing in the U.S. major leagues, but the country has dominated the annual Little League World Series. Taiwan's few forays into World Cup qualifying have been an embarrassment.

The Minnows

As many as 150 nations are eligible to compete for a place in the World Cup's final round. For many, it's a wonder they bother.

1. LUXEMBOURG

The grand duchy of Luxembourg, a country of 437,000 people in an area about the size of Rhode Island, has to be given credit for trying. Its national soccer team has entered every World Cup qualifying round since 1934 despite a long string of discouraging failures. Luxembourg's qualifying record through 1998 is two wins, two draws, and 80 defeats in 84 matches with 41 goals scored and 280 against. The country lost 32 matches in a row between 1973 and 1989, ending with a 1–1 tie versus Belgium. Luxembourg's only victories were against Portugal by a 4–2 count in 1961 and against Turkey by a 2–0 score in 1973.

2. NEPAL

Mount Everest is located in Nepal, but the country hasn't gotten above sea level in international soccer competition.

Nepal took a dive into the World Cup pool for the 1986, 1990, and 1998 events, posting a 0-14-2 record and getting outscored 58–2.

3. **MALTA**

An island nation in the center of the Mediterranean Sea, Malta has only 120 square miles of territory and a population of 391,000. A British possession, Malta was exposed to soccer during the nineteenth century but has had few successes. In World Cup qualifying play through 1998, Malta has only one win, 47 losses, and four draws while being outscored 165–17.

4. **PAKISTAN**

Pakistan's attempts to qualify for the 1994 and 1998 World Cups saw the national team succumb in all 12 matches by a combined 58–5 score.

5. **MACAO**

Macao consists of an enclave, a peninsula, and two small islands at the mouth of the Xi (Pearl) River in China. It has an area of only six square miles and a population of 450,000. Macao's foray into qualifying for the final rounds in 1994 and 1998 World Cups has resulted in a 1-10-1 record. The country was outscored 74–4.

6. **FAROE ISLANDS**

A semi-autonomous Danish possession located north of Scotland between Iceland and Norway with a population of only 45,000, the Faroe Islands participated in their first official international match in 1990. The debut resulted in a stunning 1–0 win over Austria in a game played in Sweden because there were no grass fields in the Faroe Islands. The flukish nature of the victory was underscored when Faroe Islands entered qualifying for the 1994 World Cup and lost all 10 matches while being outscored 38–1.

7. ST. VINCENT AND THE GRENADINES

A 130-square-mile volcanic island in the east Caribbean, St. Vincent and the Grenadines gained independence from Great Britain in 1979. The country of 115,000 people entered qualifying for the 1994, 1998, and 2002 tournaments, only to lose all 18 matches, scoring six goals while surrendering 84.

8. SAN MARINO

Formally known as the Most Serene Republic of San Marino, the country has a population of 27,000 and covers only 20 square miles in north central Italy near the Adriatic coast. Naturally, tiny San Marino's two attempts at reaching the World Cup final round amidst the soccer powers of Europe haven't been resounding successes. In 20 qualifying matches for the 1994 and 1998 tournaments, San Marino was outscored 90–2 while losing 19 of 20 matches. The only point that San Marino earned was in a 0–0 draw with Turkey.

9. LIECHTENSTEIN

The principality of Liechtenstein boasts only 32,000 residents over 537 mountainous square miles in the Alps between Switzerland and Austria. Its national soccer team entered World Cup play in 1998 and lost all 10 matches by an aggregate score of 52–3.

10. **MALDIVES**

A group of 19 atolls with 1,190 islands—198 of them inhabited—Maldives is located in the Indian Ocean southwest of India. It has a population of about 300,000 and is one of the world's poorest countries. During 1998 World Cup qualifying, the Maldives national soccer team was outscored 59–0 in six matches. Included was a 17–0 loss to Iran, the worst defeat in the history of men's World Cup competition at the time. Maldives also lost twice by identical 12–0 scores to Syria, which is hardly one of the globe's great soccer powers.

The Other Majors

B esides the World Cup, soccer championships are decided in a sometimes bewildering series of major tournaments staged all over the planet.

1. THE EUROPEAN CHAMPIONSHIPS

The most prestigious tournament outside the World Cup, the European championships have been played every four years since 1960. It is officially known as the European Football Championships. The Soviet Union won the first one, and in the 11 tournaments held so far, eight different countries have captured the hotly contested trophy. The Germans have won three times, twice as West Germany (1972 and 1980) and again in 1996 after reunification. France is the only other nation with multiple victories, taking home titles in 1984 and 2000.

2. COPA AMERICA

The championship of South America has been held irregularly since 1916. Argentina and Uruguay have each won 14 times. Despite its World Cup success, Brazil has won the Copa America only six times but has been victorious in three of the six championships played since 1991. Paraguay and Peru are the other multiple winners with two each.

3. AFRICAN NATIONS CUP

The championship of Africa has been held every two years since 1957. The first tournament was held in Sudan, which gained independence from Great Britain only a year earlier and built a 30,000-seat stadium for the occasion. Only Egypt and Ethiopia entered teams that year, and Egypt won both matches. Since then, the tournament has grown to include nearly every country on the continent and is an important source of national pride. Multiple winners are Egypt and Ghana (4), Cameroon and Congo/Zaire (3), and Nigeria (2).

4. CONCACAF GOLD CUP

The CONCACAF Gold Cup has been contested 13 times on an irregular basis since 1963. Mexico leads with six victories. The United States won in 1991.

5. EUROPEAN CUP/CHAMPIONS LEAGUE

The European Cup had been contested annually since the 1955–56 season by the league club champions of the member countries of the Union of European Football Associations (UEFA). In 1999, the UEFA announced the formation of a new competition called the UEFA Champions League to take the place of the Cup competition. The newly devised Champions League is a 72-team tournament with teams ranked based upon how they finished in their domestic leagues. Real Madrid of Spain won the first five tournaments and has been victorious a record eight times in all. Other multiple winners include Italy's AC Milan (5), Holland's Ajax

Amsterdam (4), England's Liverpool (4), Germany's Bayern Munich (3), Portugal's Benfica (2), Italy's Inter Milan (2), Italy's Juventus (2), and England's Nottingham Forest (2).

6. EUROPEAN'S CUP WINNER'S CUP

This competition had been contested annually by the cup winners of the member countries of the UEFA since the 1960–61 season. The Cup Winner's Cup was absorbed by the Champion's League Cup in 2000. Multiple winners include Spain's Barcelona (4), Italy's AC Milan (2), Belgium's RSC Anderlecht (2), England's Chelsea (2), and the Soviet Union's Dynamo Kiev (2).

7. UEFA CUP

The UEFA Cup has been played since the 1957–58 season by teams other than league champions and cup winners of the UEFA. Teams selected by the UEFA are based on each country's previous performance in the tournament. In 1999, with the formation of the new Champions League, the UEFA announced that the UEFA Cup would be expanded and include any teams that normally would have played in the Cup Winner's Cup. The UEFA began in 1955 as the International Industries Fairs Inter-Cities Cup, more commonly called the Fairs Cup. It was established as a tournament for the cities of Europe that sponsored industrial fairs.

8. COPA LIBERTADORES

The Copa Libertadores (Liberators' Cup) is the club championship of South America and has been played annually since 1960. Multiple winners include Argentina's Independiente (7), Uruguay's Penarol (5), Argentina's Estudiantes (3), Uruguay's

Nacional (3), Argentina's Boca Juniors (2), Brazil's Cruzeiro (2), Brazil's Gremio (2), Paraguay's Olimpia (2), Brazil's Santos (2), Brazil's Sao Paulo (2), and Argentina's River Plate (2).

9. TOYOTA CUP

Also known as the International Cup, the Toyota Cup is played annually between the winners of the European Champions League (formerly European Cup) and the Copa Libertadores. It has been played since 1960 and until 1979 was a two-game, total-goals-scored format, with each team playing one home game. The series had a reputation as a battleground for European–South American bitterness and degenerated into brutal and bloody matches with partisan fan violence a regular feature. In 1980, Toyota sponsored the competition and the championship was moved to a one-game winner-take-all match in Tokyo.

10. WOMEN'S WORLD CUP

The women's World Cup championship began in 1991 and is played every four years. The United States won in both 1991 and 1999, with Norway capturing the title in 1995.

Going for the Gold

Soccer in the Olympics has lost much of its luster because of disputes over professionalism, but the tournament has produced some extraordinary moments.

1. DENMARK, 1908

The Danes walloped France 17–1 in London with Sophus Nielsen scoring 10 goals to set an international record for one game which still stands. One of Nielsen's teammates was Niels Bohr, who went on to win the Nobel Prize for physics in 1922.

2. HAROLD WALDEN, 1912

Harold Walden scored 11 of England's 15 goals during a gold-medal-winning run in Stockholm in 1912. He later became a popular music-hall comedian in West Yorkshire.

3. BELGIUM, 1920

Belgium hosted and won the gold medal in 1920, defeating three opponents by a combined score of 15–1. In the final in Antwerp, Belgium faced Czechoslovakia, a nation newly formed from the Versailles Treaty ending World War I. Two hours before kickoff, the stadium was filled to its capacity of 40,000. One group of enterprising youths dug a tunnel under the fence to gain admission. A chain of Belgian army troops surrounded the field to keep fans from interfering with the match. With six minutes remaining in the first half and Belgium leading 2–0, English referee John Lewis sent off Czech star Karel Steiner for rough play. The entire Czech team walked off the field in protest and was disqualified.

4. URUGUAY, 1924

With frequent long-range travel between Europe and South America not yet established, Uruguay arrived at the 1924 Olympics in Paris as a virtual unknown. In their first practice sessions, the Uruguayans intentionally tripped over the ball and performed a comedy routine worthy of The Three Stooges. The European teams pledged to go easy on the poor relations from South America. In its first match, Uruguay walloped an overconfident Yugoslavia 7–1 and became the first non-European team to win a gold medal by outscoring the opposition 20–2 in five matches. Uruguay won the gold medal again in Amsterdam in 1928.

5. YUGOSLAVIA, 1960

Yugoslavia tied Bulgaria in group play which decided entry into the semifinals, and the deadlock was decided by a coin flip. Yugoslavia went on to win the gold, defeating Denmark 3–1 in the medal match.

6. PERU, 1964

The worst soccer disaster in history was the result of an Olympic qualifying match. On May 24, 1964, Peru and

Argentina met in Lima, Peru, to decide which team would go to the Olympics in Tokyo. Argentina led 1–0 with two minutes to play when Peru put the ball into the net. The goal was disqualified by Uruguayan referee Angel Eduardo Payos because of rough play by Peru. Two spectators attacked Payos and were arrested, further inflaming the passions of the crowd. Payos ordered the game suspended because of inadequate police protection. The police tried to herd the crowd out of the stadium by firing shots and tear gas into the air, but the gates were locked. Fans set the stands on fire, fighting spilled into the streets, and martial law was declared. When it was over, 328 were dead.

7. HUNGARY VS. POLAND, 1972

The 1972 Olympics final in Munich was played in a torrential rain and near gale-force winds. Hungary led 1–0 at the half, and after the teams switched sides, Poland took advantage of the wind and won 2–1.

8. SPAIN, 1992

Olympic host Spain didn't allow a goal in its first five games, a streak which ended near the end of the first half of the gold-medal contest when Poland scored before 95,000 in Barcelona. After Juan Carlos, the King of Spain, entered the stadium, the inspired Spaniards scored twice within ten minutes to take a 2–1 lead. Poland tied the score 2–2 in the 76th minute. With 52 seconds left in regulation, Spain scored off a corner kick drilled into the net by Francisco Narvaez for a 3–2 victory.

9. NIGERIA, 1996

Nigeria entered the 1996 Olympics in turmoil. After South African president Nelson Mandela criticized Nigerian dictator

Sani Abacha for hanging political dissidents, Nigeria refused to play in the African Nations Cup. The FIFA threatened to ban Nigeria from international competition but relented. The team had only a handful of practices because of endless wrangling over who would play on the team. In group play, Nigeria struggled to beat Hungary and Japan and lost 1–0 to Brazil. In the semifinals, Nigeria played Brazil again and trailed 3–1 with 20 minutes remaining. The only Nigerian goal was kicked by a Brazilian defender, and Nigeria missed a penalty kick. The Nigerians rallied to tie 3–3 in the final minute of regulation, however, and won 4–3 four minutes into sudden-death overtime. In the gold-medal game in Athens, Georgia, Nigeria was down 2–1 against Argentina with 17 minutes left and came back to win 3–2, the final goal being scored with two minutes remaining in regulation.

10. **U.S. WOMEN, 1996**

The U.S. won the first gold medal ever awarded in women's soccer in 1996 in Athens, Georgia. The Americans won the semis 2–1 against Norway 10 minutes into sudden-death overtime when Shannon MacMillan, who had entered the game as a substitute four minutes earlier, scored on a pass from Julie Foudy. Then, in the gold-medal match, the U.S. defeated China 2–1. The tie-breaking goal was scored in the second half by Tiffeny Milbrett on a pass from Joy Fawcett.

The World's Great Stadiums

The largest stadiums in the world were built as soccer venues. There are dozens that can hold more than 100,000, although the number of such venues is gradually diminishing. Maracana Stadium in Rio de Janeiro, Brazil, has a present capacity of 165,000 and at one time held 220,000. Even countries without significant international success in soccer have large stadiums. Rungnado in Pyongyang, North Korea, can hold 150,000, and Salt Lake in New Delhi, India, 120,000. Because of crowd-control problems, however, the latest trend has been to construct smaller, all-seat stadiums and to reduce the capacity of existing structures. Stadium terraces, where people stood packed like sardines in a fenced area, are being eliminated in many countries.

1. NOU CAMP IN BARCELONA, SPAIN

Nou Camp, which means "new ground," was financed in 1957 by FC Barcelona and holds 109,815. The club has continued with improvements and expansion in an effort to outdo arch rival Real Madrid. Nou Camp features an indoor sports hall, connected by a concourse, which opened in 1971 for basketball, handball, and volleyball, plus an Ice Palace and a 16,500-seat stadium for FC Barcelona's reserve team in the Spanish Second Division as well as the club's top amateur squad. For the 1992 Olympic Games, two more tiers of seating were installed above the previous roofline with a suspended cantilevered roof overhead.

2. SANTIAGO BERNABEU IN MADRID, SPAIN

The home to Real Madrid, Santiago Bernabeu opened in 1947 and currently has a capacity of 87,000. It's located on the Paseo de la Castellana, Madrid's most prestigious street, and was the site of the 1982 World Cup final. Real Madrid's previous stadium was ravaged by the Spanish Civil War. Santiago Bernabeu was the Real Madrid president who envisioned the stadium and raised the money necessary to build it by public subscription.

3. OLYMPIC STADIUM IN MUNICH, GERMANY

Built for the 1972 Olympics, this stadium is the home of the Bayern Munich soccer club and holds 63,000. It hosted the World Cup final in 1974. The Olympic Stadium is a stunning piece of architecture with a futuristic steel-and-glass web resembling a spider's web.

4. AZTECA IN MEXICO CITY, MEXICO

Holding 106,000, Azteca was built for the 1968 Olympics and is the only stadium to host two World Cup men's finals, being granted the honor in both 1970 and 1986. Despite its size, Azteca retains some intimacy because the lower level is only 13 feet from the sidelines. The stadium is the home to Mexico's America club and is also used by Altante, Nexaca, and Cruz Azul for important matches.

5. HAMPDEN PARK IN GLASGOW, SCOTLAND

In 1908, Glasgow had the three largest stadiums in the world with Hampden Park, Celtic Park, and Ibrox Stadium. Hampden Park was the largest stadium in the world until Maracana was built in 1950. On April 17, 1937, 149,415 fans paid to see Scotland defeat England, a record for a match in Europe. Seven days later, 147,365 paid to see the Celtic defeat Aberdeen 2–1 in the Scottish Cup, a European club record. In 1960, 135,000 attended the European Cup final in which Real Madrid won its fifth consecutive title by walloping Eintracht Frankfurt 7–3. Hampden Park was totally redesigned into a modern, all-seat stadium during the 1990s and reopened in 1999 with a capacity of 52,208.

6. LUZHNIKI STADIUM IN MOSCOW, RUSSIA

Luzhniki Stadium was built in 1956 and is the center of the largest sports complex in the world. It has 140 separate areas for sports, including 11 soccer fields, four tracks, three skating rinks, and 55 tennis courts. Luzhniki has a current capacity of 80,840.

7. CENTENARIO IN MONTEVIDEO, URUGUAY

Centenario was built for the first World Cup in 1930 and to honor the 100th anniversary of Uruguay's independence from Spain. It was barely completed in time as shifts worked 24 hours a day for weeks to have the facility ready for the final between Uruguay and Argentina. With a capacity of 73,609, Centenario is currently the home of the Nacional and Penarol soccer clubs.

8. STUDIO GIUSSEPPE MEAZZA IN MILAN, ITALY

The stadium is usually known by its original name of San Siro and holds 85,847. The home for AC Milan and Internazionale Milan, it was built in 1926 and underwent a major overhaul for the 1990 World Cup, which included a large overhanging roof. The renovation has been hailed as a brilliant architectural achievement, and few stadiums can match San Siro for intimacy and atmosphere. The roof has caused problems on the field, however. Neither rain nor sun can penetrate the field often enough to allow grass to take root, and, coupled with Milan's foggy, misty weather, playing conditions are usually muddy.

9. ROSE BOWL IN PASADENA, CALIFORNIA

The Rose Bowl is the only stadium in the world to host both a men's and women's World Cup final. It was also the location for the Olympic final in 1984. Built for college football's annual New Year's Day Rose Bowl game in 1922, the stadium holds more than 100,000. Three capacity crowds for the two semifinals and the final in the Olympics went a long way toward gaining the United States the right to host the 1994 World Cup.

10. WEMBLEY IN LONDON, ENGLAND

Privately owned Wembley was built in 1923 with two distinctive white towers and has long been the mecca of English soccer, revered throughout the world. It hosted the

Olympic soccer final in 1948 and the World Cup in 1966. The stadium also staged greyhound racing, rugby, and American football. It was remodeled in the 1980s with a $90,000,000 refurbishing that reduced the capacity from 126,000 to 80,000. The fabled stadium was dismantled beginning late in 2000, however, and a new Wembley is being built for $456,000,000 with a scheduled completion date of March 2003. It will feature 90,000 seats, a roof which partially retracts, and a 400-foot-high arch.

Fixer-Uppers

M any of the world's soccer stadiums of the past and present have had their share of problems.

1. MARACANA STADIUM, RIO DE JANEIRO, BRAZIL

For most of its history, Maracana would have to be listed among the world's great stadiums, but during the 1990s, it degenerated into a fetid, rat-infested dump. The world's largest stadium with a present-day capacity of 165,000, Maracana was built in 1950 for the World Cup. Today, the smell of beer and urine permeates the stadium, and it was closed twice, once after three spectators were killed when a portion of the stands collapsed. Fans had urinated on the inside walls so often that the corrosion threatened the stability of the structure. An eight-man crew was hired in 2000 to prevent the practice and send offenders to the proper facilities.

2. OLYMPIC STADIUM IN BERLIN, GERMANY

Berlin's Olympic Stadium is notorious for Adolf Hitler's propaganda exercise at the 1936 games, and the excesses of the Nazi regime still haunt the facility. For most of its lifetime, the stadium has been underused because of its political history. It was here that Jesse Owens won four gold medals in track and field events to challenge the myth of Aryan superiority. In 1938, England's soccer team was forced to give the Nazi salute before thrashing Germany 6–3. Olympic Stadium was rebuilt after being damaged by Allied bombs during World War II and renovated again for the 1974 World Cup. Another remodeling which began in 2000 will reduce the capacity from 76,342 to 52,000.

3. EASTER ROAD STADIUM IN EDINBURGH, SCOTLAND

For decades, the Scottish club Hibernian in Edinburgh played on the Easter Road Stadium field, which was sloped so that one goal was two yards lower than the other, giving the team moving downhill an advantage. It was finally leveled in 2000.

4. START STADIUM IN KIEV, UKRAINE

The day the Respublikanski Stadium in Kiev, Ukraine, was due to be inaugurated in 1941, the Nazis invaded and destroyed it. Start Stadium was saved, but it wasn't known until 1997 that the German army planted mines on the field. The anti-infantry mines were discovered about four feet below ground during renovation work in the corner of the field. They were detonated in a nearby vacant field by demolition experts.

5. VALLEY PARADE IN BRADFORD, ENGLAND

A flash fire killed 56 people, many of them children and the elderly, at Valley Parade in Bradford, England, on May 11, 1985. The official cause of the blaze was a cigarette igniting trash under the stands, but many believe the fire was started by a smoke bomb exploded by fans. The rear exits were padlocked, which contributed to the high death toll. Victims were caught between the burning roof and the burning floor of the 77-year-old structure. Fueled by a stiff breeze and plastic seats made of flammable polypropylene, the blaze burned the stands to the ground in four minutes. Steel had been delivered to build a new roof, but construction had been delayed until after the season was over. The fire occurred during Bradford's last home game of the season.

6. IBROX STADIUM IN GLASGOW, SCOTLAND

The stands collapsed at Ibrox Stadium on January 1, 1971, during the traditional New Year's Day match between the Celtic and the Rangers. Ranger supporters leaving the stadium heard the roar of the crowd and tried to turn back when the tying goal in the 1−1 draw was scored. A barrier collapsed, and fans piled on top of each other. Most of the 66 people who died were victims of suffocation. Ibrox once held 120,000 fans but has been remodeled into a 50,500 all-seat facility.

7. THE DEN IN LONDON, ENGLAND

The Den is the name given to two stadiums that have been used by the Millwall club, which has England's most notorious fan following—a notable distinction in a country plagued by hooliganism. Steve Rushin of *Sports Illustrated* wrote that "the signature song of Millwall backers goes 'no one likes us, we don't care' and there is evidence to support both sides of that claim." The old Den, used until 1993, was located in south London on the appropriately named Cold Blow Lane. According to Simon Inglis in *The Football Grounds of Great Britain,* Cold Blow Lane "might be the perfect setting for a

Jack the Ripper horror film." The new Den a few blocks away is a modern structure, but Millwall's backers still intimidate rival fans.

8. ETON COLLEGE IN ENGLAND

The Duke of Wellington commented that the Battle of Waterloo was won "on the playing fields of Eton," but the sport was banned at the fashionable school in 1959 by headmaster Robert Briley. The school's 26 soccer fields were as hard as concrete after weeks of drought, and 35 students had been treated for broken bones. The ban remained in force until the fields were softened by rain.

9. WESTFALEN STADIUM IN DORTMUND, WEST GERMANY

The stadium in Dortmund, West Germany, used for 1974 World Cup matches involving Sweden, the Netherlands, Brazil, and Bulgaria overlooked a nudist camp, much to the distraction of both the spectators and members of the clothes-optional community.

10. FURIANI STADIUM IN BASTIA, CORSICA

Before a French Cup match between the local team and Olympique Marseilles at Furiani Stadium in Bastia, Corsica, on May 5, 1992, temporary bleachers collapsed, killing 14 people. Some 10,000 temporary seats had been added to the 8,500-seat facility because of the popularity of Olympique Marseilles, then one of the strongest teams in Europe. As a result of the tragedy, FIFA banned temporary seating for all future matches.

Great Leagues of Europe

The clubs and leagues of Europe have always been the home of most of the world's great players.

1. ENGLAND

England's Premier League is the richest in the world and will grow richer with the signing of a new TV deal in 2000. Impressive new stadiums are being built, replacing aging and dangerous Victorian-era structures, as England tries to rebound from its notorious association with the hooligan element. As with major-league baseball in the United States, there are worries that the league is becoming too successful as the gap between the best and worst teams continues to grow wider because of uneven sources of revenue. The Premier League contains 20 teams, with First, Second, and Third Divisions of similar size. The bottom three teams in the standings are relegated to a lower division at the end of the season, which runs from August to May, while the top three teams in the divisions move up. The bottom three teams in the Third Division fall to the Conference, a semipro outfit. The FA Cup is the oldest national cup competition in the world. Around 600 teams from the lowest ranks of the amateur level to the

Premier League begin play in knockout rounds in August.
The championship has traditionally been played in Wembley
Stadium in May. Almost every other nation in Europe has
copied England's cup format in some manner.

2. ITALY

Italy has soccer's most passionate and knowledgeable fans.
The top level is Serie A. The teams that have had recent success and/or long, storied histories are AC Milan (Milan), Internazionale (Milan), also known as Inter Milan, Juventus (Turin),
Torino (Turin), Sampdoria (Genoa), Roma (Rome), Lazio (Rome),
Fiorentina (Florence), and Napoli (Naples). At the end of the
season, the bottom four teams in Serie A change places with
the top four in Serie B.

3. SPAIN

Soccer in Spain gained new recognition in 2000 when the
European Champions League produced an all-Spanish final
as Real Madrid defeated Valencia 3–0. FC Barcelona also
reached the semifinals, giving Spain three clubs among the
final four survivors of the tournament. Top Spanish clubs are
Real Madrid (Madrid), Real Zaragoza (Zaragoza), FC Barcelona (Barcelona), Deportivo La Coruna (La Coruna), Valencia
(Valencia), and Athletic Bilbao (Bilbao). Real Madrid is one of
Europe's most storied clubs, having won a record eight European club championships, including five in a row from 1956
through 1960.

4. GERMANY

Average crowds for league matches in Germany are the
highest in Europe. The league, known as the *Bundesliga,* consists of two divisions with 18 teams in each. The best clubs

are Bayern Munich (Munich), Borussia Dortmund (Dortmund), Bayer Leverkusen (Leverkusen), and Hertha Berlin (Berlin).

5. **FRANCE**

The French league is called *La Ligue Nationale.* The top level is the First Division, which has 18 teams. The top clubs are Girondins de Bordeaux (Bordeaux), Olympique Marseilles (Marseilles), Paris Saint-Germain (Paris), and AC Monaco (Monaco).

6. **THE NETHERLANDS**

Holland's premier league *(Eredivisie)* is dominated by Ajax Amsterdam (Amsterdam), Feyenoord (Rotterdam), and PSV Eindhoven (Eindhoven). A high income tax has made it difficult for the Netherlands to keep top domestic players from playing elsewhere.

7. **NORWAY**

Norway's 14-team premier division is called the *Tippeliga,* which Rosenborg BK (Trondheim) dominated with nine league titles during the 1990s. Matches in the north of Norway are played 200 miles above the Arctic circle, and in the land of the midnight sun lights are often unnecessary for night games.

8. **PORTUGAL**

Portugal will host the 2004 European championships, and though the country has a legion of soccer fanatics, it has trouble hanging on to top talent because of the lure of large contracts offered by clubs in England, Italy, and Germany. Dominant clubs are Benfica (Lisbon), Boavista (Oporto), and FC Porto (Oporto).

9. **RUSSIA**

Soccer in Russia is struggling to adjust from a communist economy to capitalism. An unfortunate criminal "Mafia-style" element has taken a foothold, and corruption is rampant. Spartak (Moscow) is the leading club.

10. **SCOTLAND**

There were 12 teams in the Scottish Premier League in 2000–01, but the Rangers and Celtic in Glasgow are the only ones that really matter. The two have combined to win every league championship since 1986.

Americans Abroad

One indication of the improvement in U.S. soccer is the number of players who have been signed by clubs in Europe. The success of some of the early U.S. players has prompted many of Europe's top clubs to look across the Atlantic for talent over the last five years.

1. ERIC WYNALDA

In 1992, Eric Wynalda became the first U.S. player to perform in Germany's elite Bundesliga when he inked a contract with FC Saarbrucken. Wynalda had three successful seasons in Germany before returning home to play in MLS.

2. ALEXI LALAS

With his trademark long red hair and goatee, Alexi Lalas was the first American to play in Italy's Serie A. He was with Padua in 1994–95.

3. COBI JONES

Before becoming one of the top players in MLS, Cobi Jones played for Coventry City in England in 1994–95. In 2000, he played in his 131st international match, a record for U.S. men.

4. **CLAUDIO REYNA**

In 1999, Claudio Reyna became the first American to play in soccer's holy war, the match-up between Celtic and Rangers in Glasgow, Scotland. Before joining the Rangers, Reyna was a member of Bayer Leverkusen in Germany.

5. **JOVAN KIROVSKI**

The Escondido, California, native was a member of Manchester United's youth and reserve teams from 1992 through 1996. In 1997, he became the first American to score a goal in the European Champions League while playing for Germany's Borussia Dortmund. He now plays for Sporting Lisbon.

6. **KASEY KELLER**

Goalkeeper Kasey Keller played nine seasons in England for Millwall and Leicester City. In 2001, he went to Spain to join Rayo Vallecano.

7. **JOHN HARKES**

In 1993, John Harkes became the first American to play in England's FA Cup final while in his third season with Sheffield Wednesday. His club defeated Arsenal 2–1 in overtime.

8. **JOE-MAX MOORE**

Forward Joe-Max Moore joined English powerhouse Everton in 1999.

9. **BRAD FRIEDEL**

Goalkeeper Brad Friedel became the first American to start regularly for a high-profile European club when he signed with Liverpool in 1997.

10. **FRANKIE HEJDUK**

A free spirit with long flowing hair, Frankie Hejduk was kicked off the U.S. national team in 1996 for missing a flight to China but came back to play in the 1998 World Cup. In 1999, he joined Bayer Leverkusen.

Great Clubs of England

No clubs in the world have the name recognition of those in England.

1. ARSENAL

Arsenal was the first club in London to turn professional. It has an unchallenged run of longevity in the Premier League, which dates from 1919, but the club's origins were humble, to say the least. Arsenal's first game was played on a field that had an open sewer running through it. Then the club switched to a former pig farm on the edge of a marsh. In 1913, the club moved to Highbury in North London and adopted the name Arsenal. Highbury Stadium rises from the Victorian terraced housing in London's inner city. The marbled east and west ends were built in the 1930s in Art Deco style. The north bank of the stadium was rebuilt after being destroyed by German aircraft during World War II.

2. ASTON VILLA

Aston Villa was founded in 1874 by young, faithful members of the Villa Cross Wesleyan Chapel in the North Birmingham suburb of Aston. Founding members were cricket players looking for a winter game to occupy themselves. Aston Villa was the first giant of English soccer, winning six league championships and five FA Cups between 1884 and 1913. While league titles have been hard to come by since the Victorian era, Aston Villa is still a force in the Premier League.

3. MANCHESTER UNITED

The most famous name among the English soccer teams, Manchester United was founded in 1878 as the Newton Heath Football Club in the Newton Heath suburb of Manchester by workers employed at the Lancashire and Yorkshire Railway Company. Newton Heath turned professional in 1885 but went bankrupt in 1902 and reformed as Manchester United. In 1910, the club moved to the dockside sector of the city next to the ship canal at Trafford. Manchester United gained worldwide fame with championship-caliber clubs during the 1940s and 1950s and reached its peak in 1958. But then the team was decimated by a plane crash in Munich, Germany, that killed eight players. To this day, the clock outside the club offices at Manchester United's Old Trafford Stadium remains at 3:40, the time the plane crashed. The club came back to win the league championship in 1965 and 1967 and the European Cup in 1968. The club experienced another revival during the 1990s. Manchester United won six league titles between 1993 and 2000 and another European Cup (Champions League) in 1999.

4. TOTTENHAM HOTSPUR

Tottenham Hotspur was founded in 1882 by the members of the Hotspur Cricket Club in the North London suburb of Tottenham. The name "hotspur" was taken from the nickname of well-known fifteenth-century aristocrat Harry Percy, whose titled family, the Northumberlands, owned much of Tottenham during the Middle Ages. The "Spurs" became the first British club to win a European trophy when they won the European Cup Winner's Cup in 1963. In 1972, they won the inaugural UEFA Cup.

5. CHELSEA

Winners of the FA Cup in 1970, 1997, and 2000, Chelsea is known for its glamorous supporters and scads of foreign-born players. During the 1960s and 1970s when "Swinging London" was at its peak, Chelsea was the favorite club of some of England's best-known pop stars and actors. Close to the trendy boutiques and art galleries of King's Road, Chelsea's Stamford Bridge home is located in the chic and fashionable area of central southwest London. Built in 1904, Stamford Bridge was one of the finest stadiums of its day, but by the 1980s, it was voted the worst in London. At one time or another, Stamford Bridge was used for cycling, rugby, baseball, auto racing, and greyhound racing. A new Stamford Bridge rose in its place during the 1990s in conjunction with a complex of hotels, penthouse suites, shops, bars, and restaurants. The field is scientifically laid out according to the precise microclimate of that section of London.

6. EVERTON

Everton was founded in 1878 as the Sunday school team of St. Domingo Methodist Church in the Everton District of Liverpool. They began to play in Stanley Park on Anfield Road in 1884 on a site owned by brewer John Houlding. After Everton won the league championship in 1891,

Houlding doubled the rent and insisted on retaining all of the concession revenue. A group of members led by St. Domingo organist George Mahon moved to a new ground on the other side of Stanley Park. Houlding then founded the Liverpool football club, starting a bitter rivalry that has lasted for more than 100 years. Everton is also known as the Toffeemen, because a nineteenth-century candy shop owner threw toffees to the ground before games to promote his product. Although the candy shop went out of business long ago, the tradition of throwing toffees remains.

7. **LIVERPOOL**

Liverpool had an incredible run of success with 15 league championships between 1964 and 1990. The run was marred by two tragedies, however. The first was the result of hooliganism which left 39 dead at the 1985 European Cup finals against Juventus in Belgium. And in 1989, 96 Liverpool fans died at an FA Cup final against Nottingham Forest at Hillsborough Stadium in a crush of spectators against a steel fence.

8. **WEST HAM UNITED**

London's West Ham United started as the company team of the Thames Ironworks in 1895 and is still known as the "Hammers" and the "Irons." West Ham has had solid, stable clubs but few championships. The club has yet to win a Premier League title, but they have won three FA Cups, the last in 1980.

9. **NEWCASTLE UNITED**

Located in the northeast corner of England, Newcastle United hasn't won a league championship since 1927 or an FA Cup since 1955, but during the 1990s it has not only become one the top clubs of England, but one the European elite as well. At the beginning of the decade, Newcastle was struggling in the Second Division, but aggressive management has turned the tide.

10. **LEEDS UNITED**

The pride of Yorkshire and Premier League champions in 1992, Leeds United has one of England's biggest hooligan problems. The nadir was reached in 1986 against Bradford City when Leeds fans tried to recreate the tragic Valley Parade fire, which killed 56, by setting fire to a concession stand.

Origins

M any clubs in the British Isles have unusual origins to their names.

1. ARSENAL

Arsenal was founded in 1886 by the predominately Scottish munitions employees of the Royal Arsenal installation in Woolrich, South London, in 1886.

2. CRYSTAL PALACE

Among the clubs represented at the first meeting of the England Football Association at the Freemasons' Tavern in London in 1863 was one going by the name of Crystal Palace. It was a team founded by workers at the Crystal Palace, which was built in London's Hyde Park as the centerpiece of the Great Exhibition of 1851. The Crystal Palace team was formed in 1861 and played in the first-ever FA Cup in 1872. The team folded soon after, but a new club under the same name came into existence in 1905. By that time, a new grounds named Crystal Palace had been built, capable of holding 120,000 fans. It hosted several FA Cup finals before Wembley Stadium was built in 1923.

3. LEYTON ORIENT

Located in the Leyton section of London and founded in 1888, this team added "Orient" to its name in 1905 because one of the players worked for the Orient Steam Navigation Company.

4. NOTTINGHAM FOREST

The name associated with Robin Hood and the Merry Men was founded as the Forest Football Club in Notts County in 1865 at the Clinton Arms pub.

5. PLYMOUTH ARGYLE

Plymouth Argyle was founded as the Argyle Athletic Club. The Plymouth part is easy to understand, since Argyle was located in the town of Plymouth. The origin of the Scottish name Argyle has been lost to history. Some believe it to be derived from the long-disappeared Argyle Hotel, which stood near the club's grounds. Others subscribe to the theory that the name is a tribute to the Argyll & Sutherland Highlanders, who were stationed at Plymouth at the time and fielded a championship soccer team.

6. QUEEN'S PARK RANGERS

This nomadic team has moved 18 times, mostly in suburban northwest London, since its founding in 1885. Although known as the Queen's Park Rangers, the club has never been based in the Queen's Park neighborhood of the city despite all of the packing and unpacking. It was originally formed in a merger of the St. Jude's Institute soccer team and the Christchurch Rangers, and since most of the players resided in Queen's Park, the new club took the name Queen's Park Rangers.

7. SHEFFIELD WEDNESDAY

Sheffield Wednesday was founded in 1867 as the Wednesday Cricket Club because Wednesday was the day of the week on which its players would take the afternoon off work to practice. The club soon took up soccer in addition to cricket to keep its members active during the winter months.

8. HIBERNIAN

The Hibernian club in Edinburgh, Scotland, was founded in 1875 as the club of Scotland's Irish Catholic community. Hibernian is the Roman name for Ireland. When Celtic in Glasgow was formed in 1888, it took away half of the Hibernian players, and the club never recovered. To date, Hibernian has won only three Scottish League titles, none since 1951, while Celtic has captured the title 36 seasons and has became the favorite team of most of Scotland's Catholics.

9. HEART OF MIDLOTHIAN

Also located in Edinburgh, Heart of Midlothian was named after a dance hall in which the club was formed in 1875. The dance hall took the name from the title of a novel by Walter Scott.

10. NICKNAMES

Unlike their North American counterparts, soccer teams in Europe rarely have formal nicknames. A few of the more unusual informal nicknames in England include the Cottagers (Fulham, which plays at the stadium called Craven Cottage), the Cherries (Bournemouth, which plays at a field adjacent to a cherry orchard), the Gas (Bristol Rovers), and the Magpies (Newcastle United).

Across the Channel

Clubs on the continent of Europe also have their share of strange names and unusual origins.

1. RED STAR 93

The name sounds like it belongs to a club in one of the former communist nations of Eastern Europe, but it is located in Paris, France, and was founded by Jules Rimet in 1897. Rimet is best known as the man who became FIFA president in 1921 and organized the first World Cup tournament nine years later. Unfortunately, Rimet never revealed the origin of the name Red Star 93.

2. TENNIS BORUSSIA BERLIN

The Berlin, Germany, club was formed in 1902 from the union of a social club and the Berlin Tennis and Ping Pong Society. The new organization later took up soccer when the sport became popular in Germany during the 1910s.

3. BAYER LEVERKUSEN

Today one of Europe's most powerful clubs, Bayer Leverkusen began in 1904 in Leverkusen, Germany, as the company team of the chemical plant which gave the world Bayer Aspirin.

4. JUVENTUS

The literal translation of Juventus from Italian to English is "youth." The Turin, Italy, club was founded in 1897 by students from the wealthy Massimmo d'Azeglio Grammar School. Through 2000, Juventus has won 25 Italian League championships, 21 of them since 1950.

5. TORPEDO-LUZHNIKI/ZIL

Based in Moscow, Torpedo is named after the first Soviet-built production automobile, and until recently was sponsored by ZiL, which supplied limousines to members of the politburo. The club plays at Luzhniki Stadium.

6. LOCOMOTIV

Locomotiv is also located in Moscow. It began as Moscow's railway workers' team and plays in a stadium decorated with train motifs. There's another club called Locomotiv in Sofia, Bulgaria.

7. GRASSHOPPERS

Grasshoppers is not a nickname but the formal name of the club based in Zurich, Switzerland. It was founded in 1886 by British students, though why they chose to name the club after an insect is unknown. The name stuck, and the club is easily Switzerland's most successful team. Grasshoppers has won 24 league championships.

8. FIRST VIENNA

First Vienna is called First Vienna because it was the first all-soccer club in Vienna, Austria. It was founded by English gardeners on Baron Rothschild's estate. First Vienna plays at Hohe Warte Stadium, which was built in 1923 into a hillside on the estate.

9. DYNAMO

There are Dynamo teams (also spelled dinamo) in Moscow, Russia; Kiev, Ukraine; Bucharest, Hungary; Zagreb, Yugoslavia; Berlin, (East) Germany; and Dresden, (East) Germany. During the communist regimes of those nations, each team was controlled by the secret police, which usually made sure that its club had the best players. In East Germany, Dynamo Berlin won a world-record 10 consecutive league championships beginning in 1979, and starting in 1976, 15 league championships were won by either Dynamo Berlin or Dynamo Dresden.

10. NICKNAMES

Some of the more unusual nicknames in continental Europe include: Mattress Makers (Atletico Madrid), Kangaroos (Bohemians in Prague, Czech Republic), Soupeaters (CSKA in Sofia, Bulgaria), and Canaries (Fenerbache in Istanbul, Turkey).

Great Rivalries

There are no sports rivalries like those in soccer, many of which have elements of cultural and religious wars.

1. CELTIC VS. RANGERS IN GLASGOW, SCOTLAND

The rivalry between Celtic and Rangers is the most intense in all of Europe and symbolizes the religious antagonism between the Catholic (Celtic) and Protestant (Rangers) halves of Scottish society. The clubs also represent different sides of the city with Celtic in their traditional green uniforms on the east side and the Rangers' blue on the west. The Rangers were formed in 1873 and didn't have a Catholic player until 1988. The Celtic has long had Protestant players and coaches and was founded in 1888 by Irish Catholics in Glasgow to finance soup kitchens for the neighborhood poor.

2. REAL MADRID VS. BARCELONA IN SPAIN

The intense and explosive rivalry between Real Madrid and Barcelona is not only a competitive one between two of Spain's top teams, but a rivalry with cultural, political, and ethnic overtones as well. Real Madrid is the "royal" club of

Spain's capital, and Barcelona is the Catalan "people's" club. Independent-minded Barcelona was a center of resistance to Francisco Franco's fascists, who took over the country in the civil war in 1936 and brutally emasculated the Catalan ethnic minority in the region. Real was Franco's favorite club. Real Madrid's members include Spain's king and queen and International Olympic Committee President Juan Antonio Samarranch.

3. FLAMENGO VS. FLUMINENSE IN BRAZIL

Also known as the "Flu-Fla" rivalry, Flamengo and Fluminense are both based in Rio de Janeiro. In 1963, a clash between the two drew 177,656 fans, a world record for a club match. Flamengo is the most popular team in Brazil and was formed in 1911 by dissident members of the Fluminense club. Fluminense was founded by British residents of the city in 1902 and maintains much of its upper-crust origins. The fashion in Brazil at the beginning of the twentieth century was for the wealthy, socially exclusive class to wear white powder on their faces, and to this day Fluminense fans put white powder on their faces as a sign of loyalty. Fluminense also refused to sign blacks in multiracial Brazil until the 1950s.

4. RIVER PLATE VS. BOCA JUNIORS IN BUENOS AIRES, ARGENTINA

These clubs are the two giants of Argentine soccer. River Plate has traditionally been the team from the rich side of Buenos Aires. Boca has the support of those from the "wrong side of the tracks" and was formed by Irishman Patrick McCarthy and a group of Italian immigrants in 1905. The rivalry has been plagued by violence. On June 23, 1968, at El Estadio Monumental in Buenos Aires, Boca Juniors supporters dropped lit torches onto River Plate fans. Panic ensued, resulting in the deaths of 74 spectators.

5. NACIONAL VS. PENAROL IN URUGUAY

In Uruguay, one is born as either a Nacional fan or a Penarol fan, and the fans of both clubs have been dedicated to hating each other for 100 years. According to Eduardo Galeano in *Soccer in Sun and Shadow,* prostitutes in Uruguay used to lure customers by wearing nothing but a Nacional or Penarol shirt.

6. EVERTON VS. LIVERPOOL IN LIVERPOOL, ENGLAND

John Lennon and the Beatles hailed from Liverpool and wanted to "give peace a chance," but there's no chance of peace between the city's leading soccer clubs as Everton and Liverpool form the most bitterly intense rivalry in England. The bitterness is exacerbated by the proximity of the stadiums of the two teams. Everton's Goodison Park and Liverpool's home, Anfield Road, are on opposite sides of a public park.

7. ARSENAL VS. TOTTENHAM HOTSPUR IN LONDON, ENGLAND

Arsenal and Tottenham Hotspur are two of England's top clubs and form a bitter rivalry in North London. Arsenal moved from South London to North London in 1913 amid recriminations that Arsenal was stealing Tottenham's fans. Although things have quieted somewhat in the last decade, matches between the two clubs escalated into street battles during the 1970s and 1980s.

8. AJAX VS. FEYENOORD IN THE NETHERLANDS

Hooliganism has been a severe problem in the Netherlands as well as in England, and vicious battles between the fans of the two soccer powers have frequently taken place both in the stands and in the streets. The styles of play of the two clubs reflect the cities they represent. Feyenoord plays in Rotterdam, which sees itself as a blue-collar, hard-working city, and which considers Ajax and Amsterdam to be flashy and arrogant.

9. AC MILAN VS. INTERNAZIONALE IN MILAN, ITALY

The rivalry between AC Milan and Internazionale dates from 1908, when members of AC Milan, then known as Milan FC, broke away in protest of the British influence on the club. The new group called itself Internazionale because of the group's multinational nature. The two clubs have combined to win 22 Italian League championships since 1951, 14 of them by AC Milan.

10. OLYMPIAKOS VS. AEK IN ATHENS, GREECE

The two powers of the Greek League had so many problems with fan violence that matches during the 1980s were moved to the island of Rhodes.

Fan Culture

Fan culture in Europe varies from country to country.

1. DENMARK

As an antidote to hooliganism, many fans in Denmark declared themselves roligans (rolig means peaceful) during the 1980s. The roligans are good-natured fans who paint their faces and wear daffy Viking hats and display goodwill toward their opponents, win or lose.

2. ENGLAND

Although hooliganism is still a major issue in England, stadium designs have defused much of the problem. Much of the trouble was generated by terraces, which were standing-room-only areas where fans were packed close together like sardines. These have disappeared at all but the small Third Division venues. Some complain, however, that soccer has become too commercialized in England and that too much of the old match-day atmosphere has been lost.

3. **GERMANY**

In most German stadiums, the announcers who introduce players before the match shout out only their first names. The fans respond with the last names in unison.

4. **GREECE**

The Greeks have fallen behind the rest of the continent in stadium construction. Most Greek stadiums are no more comfortable than those of Aristotle's day. Fans still have to sit on primitive stone seats, and even the most hardy of the lot use polystyrene pillows. Fireworks are shot off from the stands throughout the matches.

5. **HOLLAND**

To counter hooliganism, Holland began admitting only club members to Premier League matches in 1996. Members are given cards, and only card holders can enter the grounds. In addition, Dutch mayors have the authority to unilaterally cancel matches if they suspect trouble. The scheme has reduced violence but hasn't completely eliminated it, especially when arch rivals Ajax Amsterdam and Feyenoord meet.

6. **ITALY**

Nowhere are soccer fans more passionate than in Italy. Fans sing, wave flags, and shout slogans in elaborate choreographed movements. Match violence is a problem but is rarer than in most European countries, in part because of a strong police presence. Traffic jams often form at the gates preceding the games because fans routinely are searched for items which can be thrown onto the field. Even coins are confiscated.

7. **SPAIN**

Fans in Spain wave white handkerchiefs for both good play and bad, a custom borrowed from bullfighting. Because of escalating violence, the Spanish FA banned alcohol from stadiums in 1990 and fireworks in 1992.

8. **SWITZERLAND**

For a country that managed to remain neutral during World War I and World War II, it's not surprising that the Swiss are Europe's least aggressive fans. Earplugs are a prerequisite, however, as the Swiss ring cowbells throughout the matches.

9. **ST. PAUL**

A small club in Hamburg, Germany, which usually struggles to win matches, St. Paul has become the favorite of the left-leaning political movement in the city. The club's stadium is located in a neighborhood of brothels and strip joints. St. Paul fans pride themselves on their anti-Nazism and anti-racism, and many root against Germany in international matches as a protest against Germany's government.

10. **ROME**

The rivalry between Lazio and Roma, Rome, Italy's, two dominant teams, is politically charged. Lazio was the favorite team of Benito Mussolini, and its fans are generally right-wing and suburban, while Roma draws from the inner-city left.

British Hooliganism

English officials in both the government and the soccer community have worked hard to eradicate the problem of hooliganism but have had little success. Foreign nations—especially their security forces—dread the arrival of England's national team or any of its clubs. Most attribute hooliganism to England's past economic problems and high industrial unemployment, the country's loss of status in the world during the twentieth century, and a right-wing, racist fringe in British society.

1. HEYSEL

Thirty-nine died at 70,000-seat Heysel Stadium in Brussels, Belgium, on May 29, 1985, before a European Cup match between Liverpool and Juventus of Turin, Italy. Most of the victims were Italian and were crushed under the weight of a stand that collapsed. The tragedy occurred because a group of Liverpool fans charged into an area reserved for supporters of Juventus. The match went on because officials feared further violence if it were called off. Juventus won 1–0. English club teams were banned from competition in Europe for five years, though the edict didn't extend to the national

team. The following August, a memorial service led by
Archbishop Derek Warlock was held before Liverpool's first
home game of the season, but it was marred because many
of the Archbishop's words were drowned out by fans shouting anti-Italian slogans. Courts in Belgium convicted 14
Englishmen of manslaughter for instigating the tragedy.

2. FERRY ACROSS THE NORTH SEA

Three people were stabbed in a brawl in 1986 among 150
fans on a North Sea ferry bound for the Netherlands from
Harwich, England. The group was planning to root for the
English national team in a match in the Netherlands, but
fans of Liverpool, Everton, and Manchester United fought
each other. Concerned by the threat to other passengers, the
captain locked the drunken contingent in the bar, turned the
ship around, and headed back to England.

3. LEEDS UNITED

Fans of Leeds United are noted not only for their violence
but their tastelessness as well. During a match against Bradford City a few months after the tragic Valley Parade blaze,
Leeds United supporters tried to recreate the event by setting fire to a concession stand.

4. THE HILLSBOROUGH TRAGEDY

In 1989, 96 people were killed at Hillsborough Stadium in
Sheffield when fans rushing into the stadium were crushed
against a wire fence. Hundreds stumbled down the terraces
shortly after the start of the FA Cup tournament game
between Liverpool and Nottingham Forest. Contributing to
the tragedy were fortified walls and high steel-frame fencing,

barriers designed to keep fans off the field and from throwing debris onto it. The incident led to the banning of the century-old tradition of terraces, and most of England's soccer stadiums were converted to all-seaters.

5. ITALY

During the 1990 World Cup, Italian officials scheduled each of England's group matches for the island of Sardinia because they believed control and deportation of hooligans would be easier from a smaller area surrounded by water.

6. PAUL SCARROTT

Paul Scarrott is representative of the worst elements of hooliganism. "I'm the world's vilest hooligan," he bragged in 1990, "and I'm proud of it." By the time he was 34 years old, he had already amassed 40 convictions for soccer-fan violence. Scarrott was barred from attending the 1990 World Cup but was hired as a correspondent by London's *Daily Star* and sneaked into Italy on a fake passport. "They'll never stop me," he boasted in a dispatch. "We're after the Dutch and we want to give them a good kicking. We'll wait for them with tear gas bombs at the Termini Station." Scarrott also said he planned to visit the Pope. He was apprehended by Italian police and sent back to England.

7. 1990 WORLD CUP

Two hours before the England-Netherlands match, 1,000 English and Dutch fans exchanged rocks and tear gas during a clash. While Italians celebrated their country's 2–0 victory over Uruguay, English fans threw bottles and smashed car windows. Police used tear gas, clubs, and rowboat oars in an effort to restore order. After riots shook the seaside town of Rimini, 500 fans from England were taken into custody and 246 expelled from Italy.

8. **REVENGE**

After England lost to Germany in the 1990 World Cup, 300 French and German students had to be locked inside a night-club in London for their own safety while English fans rampaged the city. Rioting took place all over the country, and German cars were targeted and set on fire.

9. **IRELAND**

Violence forced the referees to cancel a "friendly" between England and Ireland 27 minutes into the match on February 15, 1995, before a capacity crowd of 40,000 at Landsdowne Road in Dublin that included Ireland's President Mary Robinson. A group of English fans in the upper deck ripped up seats and threw bits of wood and metal at the people below. David Platt, a player for England, went to the stands to plea for calm but gave up after he was nearly hit by a piece of wood.

10. **NATIONAL FRONT PARTY**

During the late 1970s, England's problems with fan violence grew worse when the National Front Party, a racist, right-wing organization opposed to immigration, recruited soccer hooligans. The party urged the hooligans to attack Asian, African, and Caribbean immigrants at games, destroy property, and hurl verbal abuse toward minority players.

Fluke Goals

G oals are often the result of luck rather than design.

1. RAIMUNDO ORSI

Italy was in desperate straits during the 1934 World Cup final against Czechoslovakia in Rome. The Italians trailed 1–0 with nine minutes to play when Raimundo Orsi took a pass from Enrique Guaita, ran though the Czech defense, feinted with his left foot, and shot with his right. The ball swerved crazily, brushed goalkeeper Frantisek Planicka's fingers, and curled into the net. Italy added a goal in extra time to win the championship 2–1. In postgame interviews, reporters called it a lucky shot. Orsi indignantly said he could make that shot anytime he wanted and would prove the point. The next day, he tried to repeat the feat for photographers but was unsuccessful on 20 attempts, even though there was no goalkeeper to stop him.

2. DIEGO MARADONA

Bitter rivals Argentina and England met in the quarter-finals of the World Cup on June 22, 1986, in Mexico City. Five minutes into the second half, Diego Maradona scored the first goal of the game, at least according to the officials. Television replays showed Maradona hit the ball with his hand, but Tunisian referee Ali Bennaceur ruled that Maradona had headed the ball into the netting. Maradona scored again later in the match, brilliantly dribbling nearly half the length of the field through four English defenders. Argentina won 2–1. Maradona disputed claims that the ball had hit his hand even though there was visual evidence. He maintained that the ball had hit "the hand of God." Years later, however, Maradona admitted the ball had hit his hand and that the goal wasn't the result of divine intervention.

3. WOLFGANG WEBER

England was leading 2–1 in the 1966 World Cup final against Germany in injury time as fans at Wembley Stadium in London were breathlessly waiting for Swiss referee Gottfried Dienst to blow his whistle to end the game. Jack Charlton of England and Siegfried Held of Germany both leaped for a ball, and Dienst called a questionable penalty on Charlton. Lothar Emmerich took the free kick, and Wolfgang Weber knocked the ball past England goalkeeper Gordon Banks from just six yards out. Only 15 seconds after the goal, Dienst signaled the end of regulation with the score tied 2–2.

4. GEOFF HURST

Germany tied the 1966 World Cup final with a flukish controversial goal. England won it on one. Geoff Hurst's shot hit the underside of the crossbar and bounced straight down. The English players insisted the ball crossed the line. Referee Gottfried Dienst wasn't sure and consulted Russian linesman Tofik Bakhramov. After what seemed like an eternity, Dienst decided it was a goal. It was Hurst's third score of the match, making him the only player in history to net three goals in a World Cup final. England added another one in extra time and came away with a 4–2 victory and the world championship. Hurst was granted knighthood by the English government in 1998.

5. OLIVER BIERHOFF

A fluke goal won the 1996 European championship. On June 30 in London, German substitute Oliver Bierhoff posted up one Czech defender while ramming a shot off another. The ball barely trickled through the hands of the goalkeeper just over the line near the post. The score gave Germany a 2–1 win five minutes into sudden-death overtime. One of the linesmen said Bierhoff was offside, but he was overruled by the referee. Bierhoff, playing only because injuries knocked out several German players, had tied the score with a goal 22 minutes earlier.

6. JOE GAETJENS

Whether Joe Gaetjens's most famous goal was a fluke or not has long been in dispute, but there is no doubt that it produced one of the great upsets of all time. In the 1–0 victory by the United States over England in the 1950 World Cup, Gaetjens took a cross from Warren Bahr and headed it into the goal. Many claim that Gaetjens didn't even see the ball coming and that the ball hit his head by accident.

7. VILMOS SEBOK

Hungary needed a tie and Finland was required to win to advance to the final rounds of the World Cup when the two European nations met in a qualifying match on October 11,

1997, in Helsinki. During a frantic scramble in front of the net with Finland leading 1–0 during stoppage time, Vilmos Sebok of Hungary launched a desperate shot. Finland defender Sami Mahlio stretched to save it but managed only to bounce the ball off the back of goalkeeper Teuvo Moilanen's thigh, sending it into the net. Hungary had a 1–1 draw and a berth in France.

8. KLAUS HARTWIG

In a 1995 Sixth Division match in Germany between SF Larrelt and Emden, referee Klaus Hartwig "scored" a goal. Hartwig was standing outside the goal area when an Emden forward unleashed a fierce shot that was so far off target that it hit the referee in the forehead and flew into the net to tie the score 1–1. The game was delayed while Hartwig was treated with ice. Fortunately, SF Larrelt scored again and won 2–1.

9. INIGO ARTEAGA

Goalkeeper Inigo Arteaga of the Spanish club Racing Ferris became the first professional goalkeeper to score directly from a goal kick, putting his club up 2–0 against Moralo. In the 70th minute of a Third Division game on November 2, 1997, the goal kick sailed 100 yards and bounced past opposing keeper Jose Peralta.

10. GIUSEPPE MEAZZA

In the 1938 World Cup semifinals, Giuseppe Meazza of Italy scored on a penalty kick just seconds before his ripped shorts fell to his ankles in a match against Brazil. Some believe that Meazza loosened his shorts intentionally to distract the goalkeeper. The Italians won 2–1 to advance to the final.

Great Victories in Extra Time

Geoff Hurst's goal in the 1966 final isn't the only thrilling one to be scored during extra time in a major tournament.

1. ANGELO SCHIAVO, 1934

The 1934 World Cup final between Italy and Czechoslovakia in Rome was tied 1–1 after Raimundo Orsi's remarkable goal in the 80th minute. In extra time, both teams were near exhaustion. Giuseppe Meazza was hobbled by an injury, and the Czechs didn't bother to mark him. In the 95th minute, Meazza fired a pass to Enrique Guaita, who fed Angelo Schiavo near the Czech goal. Schiavo rounded a defender and launched a shot just under the crossbar, giving Italy a 2–1 victory.

2. ANTON SCHALL, 1934

Austria's Anton Schall scored the first extra-time goal in World Cup history on May 27, 1934, against France in Turin, Italy. Schall's score broke a 1–1 tie in Austria's 3–2 victory. Most observers thought Schall was obviously offside. Years later, he admitted that he probably was.

3. SILVIO PIOLA, 1938

The Italian team went to the 1938 World Cup tournament in France with an admonition from dictator Benito Mussolini that they must "win or die." Silvio Piola kept his team alive in more ways than one in the first match against Norway with an extra-time goal four minutes into the extra period for a 2–1 victory in the 16-team knockout format used in 1938. Italy won its next three matches to take the trophy. It was Norway's first final-round game in World Cup play. Norway wouldn't play another until 1994.

4. JIMMY DICKINSON, 1954

The 1954 first-round World Cup match between England and Belgium was knotted up 3–3 after 90 minutes after Belgium had scored twice in the final 15 minutes of regulation. England struck in the first minute of extra time to take a 4–3 lead, but the match ended in a 4–4 tie because Jimmy Dickinson headed a free kick into his own net.

5. MARIO KEMPES, 1978

Mario Kempes scored two goals and assisted on another to give Argentina a 3–1 win in extra time over the Netherlands in the 1978 World Cup final in Buenos Aires. He scored in the 37th minute to give Argentina a 1–0 lead and again in the 105th minute to put his country up 2–1 when he beat three men to drive the ball past Dutch goalkeeper Jan Jongbloed. Kempes also assisted on Daniel Bertoni's score in the 114th minute.

6. SANDOR KOCSIS

The 1954 World Cup semifinal between Hungary and Uruguay in Lausanne, Switzerland, had the makings of a classic matchup. Hungary was considered to be the top team in the world, and Uruguay had never lost in the World Cup final round, with 10 victories and one draw in 11 matches dating back to 1930. Sandor Kocsis scored two extra-time goals in the 112th and 117th minutes, both on headers, to give Hungary a 4–2 victory.

7. ITALY AND WEST GERMANY, 1970

In the 1970 World Cup semifinals in Mexico City, Italy and West Germany combined for five extra-time goals. Italy appeared to be on its way to victory when West Germany's Karl-Heinz Schnellinger scored in the second minute of injury time to tie the score 1–1. The five extra-time goals were scored in a span of 16 minutes. West Germany scored first before the Italians took a 3–2 lead. After West Germany evened the score, Gianni Rivera scored the game-winner to provide Italy with a 4–3 decision.

8. SOVIET UNION AND BELGIUM, 1978

In the second round of the World Cup in 1978, the Soviet Union and Belgium finished regulation tied 2–2. Belgium scored twice in extra time to lead 4–2, but the Soviets refused to give up. They scored on a penalty to make the score 4–3, and in the dying seconds, Belgian goalkeeper Jean-Marie Pfaff barely tipped a shot over the bar.

9. ROGER MILLA, 1990

Cameroon and Colombia played scoreless soccer for 105 minutes in the second round in Naples, Italy, in 1990. Roger Milla, then 38 years old, came on as a 54th-minute substitute and scored twice in the second overtime period to give Cameroon a 2–1 victory.

10. **LAUREПT BLAПC, 1998**

In 1998, the World Cup abandoned the full 30 minutes of extra time and went to a sudden-death, "golden goal" format. The first golden goal in history was scored in the second round by France's Laurent Blanc in the 113th minute to defeat Paraguay 1−0 in Lens.

Fantastic Finishes in International Matches

Many of soccer's great international matches have gone down to the wire.

1. **BRAZIL, 1962**

The Brazilians needed a win against Spain to stay alive in the 1962 World Cup in Chile but trailed 1–0. Amarildo, who was playing for an injured Pele, tied the match 1–1 in the 71st minute on a brilliant pass from Garrincha. Amarildo gave Brazil the victory in the final minute of regulation on another assist from Garrincha. Eleven days later, Brazil defeated Czechoslovakia 3–1 in the final.

2. **BULGARIA, 1993**

In the final match of World Cup qualifying on November 17, 1993, in Paris, Bulgaria needed a win to advance to the final rounds, and France required a draw. France should have wrapped up a spot in their previous match. The French had held a 2–1 lead at home against a weak team from Israel, only to lose 3–2 on two goals in the final seven minutes. France was again victimized as Bulgaria's Emil Kostadinov scored in the 90th minute for a 2–1 triumph. France recovered from the debacle, however, to win the next World Cup in 1998.

3. FRANCE, 1984

France won the European championship in 1984, aided by a late goal in the semifinal against Portugal in Marseilles. The score was 2–2 in the 120th minute and headed for penalties when Jean Tigada went on a surge down the field and crossed low to Michael Platini, who scored to win 3–2. Two days later, France beat Spain 2–0 to win the championship.

4. FRANCE, 2000

France won the European championship again in 2000 with a sensational finish. In the final against Italy at Rotterdam in the Netherlands, the Italians led 1–0 three and one-half minutes into injury time and were already clapping and giving each other high fives in anticipation of victory when Sylvan Wiltord scored to send the contest into overtime. France won the championship with a 2–1 decision on David Trezeguet's goal in the 103rd minute.

5. ENGLAND, 1990

In the second round of the 1990 World Cup, England and Belgium were tied 0–0 in the 120th minute when England scored to advance with a 1–0 victory. Paul Gascoigne was fouled and took the free kick himself. David Platt timed his run perfectly, took Gascoigne's setup, and swiveled to volley home a spectacular goal. After defeating Cameroon 3–2 in extra time in the quarterfinals, England lost to West Germany on penalty kick in the semis.

6. NORWAY, 1998

In the 1998 World Cup, Norway needed a win over powerful Brazil to advance to the second round. Trailing the Brazilians 1–0, Tore Andre Flo equalized with a goal in the 83rd minute. In the 88th minute, following a debatable foul, Norway scored on a penalty kick by Kjetil Rekdal for a 2–1 victory.

7. ARGENTINA, 1986

Argentina and West Germany were the opponents for the World Cup final on June 29, 1986, in Mexico City. Argentina took a 2–0 lead on goals in the 22nd and 55th minutes. The team couldn't hold off a West German rally, however, which produced scores in the 73rd and 81st minutes. Seven minutes from the end of regulation, Jorge Burruchaga of Argentina took a perfect pass and ran half the length of the field to beat West German goalkeeper Harald Schumacher. Argentina had a 3–2 victory and a world championship.

8. WEST GERMANY, 1970

During the 1970 World Cup quarterfinals, England led West Germany 2–0 early in the second half. England seemed set to coast into the semifinals but was playing without goalkeeper Gordon Banks, who was ill. West Germany rallied with three goals, the third by Gerd Muller in extra time to win 3–2.

9. AUSTRIA, 1954

In the 1954 World Cup quarterfinals in Lausanne, Switzerland, the Swiss thrilled the home crowd by taking a 3–0 lead after only 23 minutes. Austria amazingly came back to tie the score within three minutes and netted five goals in a 10-minute span to take a 5–3 lead. The final was Austria 7,

Switzerland 5, the highest-scoring game in World Cup final-round history.

10. **URUGUAY, 1950**

Uruguay trailed Sweden in the second round of the 1950 World Cup 2-1, but Omar Oscar Miguez struck with two quick goals, the first in the 77th minute and another five minutes from time for a 3-2 victory. The win allowed Uruguay to reach the final, where they defeated host Brazil 2-1, a team which had previously destroyed Sweden 7-1.

Fantastic Finishes in Club and College Matches

Clubs and colleges have had their share of fantastic finishes as well.

1. MANCHESTER UNITED, 1999

Manchester United became the European championship title holders on May 27, 1999, with an amazing finish against Bayern Munich in Barcelona, Spain, by scoring two goals in injury time for a 2–1 victory. Manchester United had been down 1–0 since early in the first half. Bayern Munich had numerous chances to put the game away, but they could not score another goal. Teddy Sheringham netted the tying goal and Ole Gunnar Solksjaer the winner. Both came off corners by David Beckham, and both goal scorers had entered the game as substitutes. Manchester United won the League title, the FA Cup, and the continental club championship in the same season. The only other clubs to win all three titles are Celtic Glasgow (1967), Ajax Amsterdam (1973), and PSV Eindhoven (1988).

2. NCAA FINAL FOUR, 1999

In the NCAA final four in 1999, both semifinal games went to four overtimes. On December 10 in Charlotte, North Carolina, Santa Clara defeated Connecticut 2–1 after 138 minutes and 50 seconds of playing time. Shawn Parcelli scored both goals for Santa Clara. In the second game, Indiana edged UCLA 3–2, requiring 141 minutes and 24 seconds before Ryan Mack ended the match with a score. In the championship game two days later, Indiana required only 90 minutes to beat Santa Clara 1–0.

3. CHELSEA, 1997

Player-coach Gianluca Vialli weaved through a blizzard to score two late goals for Chelsea to defeat home team Tronso of Norway 3–2 in the European Cup Winners Cup on October 23, 1997. Snow fell throughout the second half of the match, held 200 miles above the Arctic Circle. Play had to be stopped twice for the groundskeepers to sweep the lines.

4. BLACKPOOL, 1953

In the 1953 England FA Cup final, Blackpool stunned Bolton 4–3. Bolton led 3–1 before Blackpool came back. Stanley Mortensen scored Blackpool's second goal in the 68th minute and tied it in the 89th minute with a free kick. A minute later, Mortensen assisted Bill Perry on the game-winner.

5. DC UNITED, 1996

In the first Major League Soccer championship match, played on October 20, 1996, in Foxboro, Massachusetts, DC United trailed the Los Angeles Galaxy 2–0 in a torrential rain with

50-mile-per-hour winds blowing across the field. DC United stormed back with two goals in the final 17 minutes of regulation to tie the score 2–2. Three minutes into sudden-death overtime, Eddie Pope headed home a corner kick from Marco Etcheverry for DC United's 3–2 victory.

6. LIVERPOOL, 1989

England's FA Cup final in 1989 featured arch rivals Liverpool and Everton on May 20 at Wembley Stadium. Liverpool took a 1–0 lead in the fourth minute on a goal by John Aldridge which held up for 85 minutes. Everton deadlocked the match 1–1 in the 89th minute on a score from substitute John McCall on a cross from Pat Nevin. In extra time, Liverpool's sub Ian Rush scored twice, first in the 95th minute and again in the 104th minute after Everton had equalized, giving his club a 3–2 victory.

7. UCLA, 1985

In the longest-ever collegiate soccer match, UCLA defeated American University in the 1985 NCAA championship game 1–0 after 166 minutes and 5 seconds of play in Seattle. The lone goal was scored by Paul Caliguri.

8. MANCHESTER UNITED, 1968

With a pair of fantastic finishes, Manchester United became the first club from England to win the European Cup. In the semis at Wembley Stadium, Manchester United trailed Real Madrid 3–1 with 20 minutes remaining and rallied for a 4–3 win. In the final versus Benfica, "Man U" scored three goals in extra time to win 4–1.

9. NOTRE DAME, 1996

Notre Dame's women ended North Carolina's streak of nine consecutive NCAA championships by defeating the Tar Heels 1−0 in the semifinals. In the final, the Fighting Irish went to three overtimes before Cindy Daws scored off of a direct free kick in the 126th minute to defeat Portland 1−0.

10. JUVENTUS, 1982

The Italian League championship came down to the final minutes in 1982. Heading into the final day, Juventus and Fiorentina were tied for first. The two teams were playing separate matches, and if they remained tied for the top spot, a playoff would decide the title. It didn't happen. Both games were tied at halftime, but in the second half, a Fiorentina goal was disallowed, while Juventus scored in the 75th minute of their match on a disputed penalty to take the title. Nearly two decades later, it's still unwise to mention the 1981−82 season finale around Fiorentina fans.

No Way to End a Match

Due to scheduling restraints and television, FIFA switched its tiebreaker policy. Rather than replaying a match in its entirety, a penalty-kick format would decide the winner. The format was first used in the World Cup in 1982.

1. ITALY VS. BRAZIL, 1994

The only men's World Cup final to be decided by penalty kicks took place in the Rose Bowl in Pasadena, California, between Italy and Brazil in 1994. Both teams were vying for their fourth world championship. They played 120 minutes to a scoreless tie. The penalty round ended when Roberto Baggio, who had kept Italy alive with five goals in the previous three games, missed a shot which hurtled over the crossbar.

2. WEST GERMANY VS. FRANCE, 1982

The first penalty-kick shoot-out in World Cup history took place in the 1982 semifinals between West Germany and France in Seville, Spain. The match ended 1–1 after regulation and was followed by a feast of four goals in the first 17 minutes of extra time. France took a 3–1 lead by the 98th minute on scores from Marius Tresor and Alain Giresse, but it took only nine minutes for the West Germans to tie the match again 3−3 on goals by Karl-Heinz Rummenigge and Klaus Fischer. In the penalty round, each club made its first four shots before West German Harald Schumacher stopped one. Horst Hrubesch converted, and West Germany advanced to the final.

3. BRAZIL VS. THE NETHERLANDS, 1998

The Netherlands tied the score 1−1 in the 87th minute and fought off defending champion Brazil the rest of the way to force a penalty-kick shoot-out in the 1998 semifinals in France. Brazil won 4−2 in the penalty round but lost 3−0 to France in the final.

4. WEST GERMANY VS. MEXICO, 1986

West Germany and Mexico battled through 120 minutes of scoreless soccer in a quarterfinal match in Monterrey, Mexico. The home team bowed out 4−1 on penalty shots.

5. ARGENTINA VS. YUGOSLAVIA, 1990

Argentina and Yugoslavia ended extra time with a 0−0 score in the 1990 quarterfinals in Florence, Italy. Argentina missed two shots in the penalty round, including one by Diego Maradona, but Yugoslavia failed to convert three, and Argentina moved to the semifinals.

6. ARGENTINA VS. ITALY, 1990

Argentina lost its first match in 1990 in a 1−0 upset against Cameroon but advanced to the finals after defeating Yugoslavia on penalties in the quarters and host Italy in the semis. The Italy match was played in Naples and was 1–1 after 120 minutes. In extra time, the two teams seemed more interested in injuring each other than in scoring goals, and Argentina was reduced to ten men when Ricardo Giusti was red carded for a foul on Roberto Baggio. In the penalty round, Argentina's goalkeeper Sergio Javier Goyochea saved two shots, and Argentina advanced to the finals, where they lost 1–0 to West Germany.

7. ITALY VS. FRANCE, 1998

On the way to the world championship in 1998, France had to win in overtime against Paraguay in the second round and on penalty kicks versus Italy in the quarterfinals. Against Italy, the score was 0–0 after 120 minutes of intense soccer. France won 4–3 on penalties. On the final shot, French goalkeeper Fabien Barthez dove the wrong way on Luigi di Biagio's kick, but the ball hit the crossbar.

8. SWEDEN VS. ROMANIA, 1998

Sweden was down 2–1 with five minutes remaining in extra time and playing with ten men against Romania in the 1998 quarterfinals in France before tying the match and sending it to the penalty round. Sweden converted five shots to Romania's four to advance.

9. IRELAND VS. ROMANIA, 1990

In the second round in Genoa, Italy, Ireland and Romania fought to a scoreless draw after the two periods of extra time. Ireland won the penalty shoot-out 5–4, with David O'Leary converting the deciding goal.

10. **ARGENTINA VS. THE NETHERLANDS, 1998**

The Dutch eventually lost to Brazil in the 1998 semifinals on penalty kicks but needed the shoot-out in the second round to get that far. After a 2–2 tie, the Netherlands beat Argentina 4–3 on penalty kicks.

Injury Time

With its collisions, sudden stops and turns, and passionate fans, soccer has always produced its share of injuries.

1. PETER RADAKOVIC

Yugoslavia had lost to West Germany in the quarterfinals in both 1954 and 1958 and had to face the West Germans again in the quarters in the 1962 World Cup in Santiago, Chile. Yugoslavia won, advancing to the semifinals for the only time in its history. The goal was scored in the 87th minute from the edge of the penalty area by Peter Radakovic, whose head was wrapped in bandages from an injury suffered earlier in the game. Yugoslavia lost in the semis 1–0 to Chile.

2. ERNIE BRANDTS

Ernie Brandts of the Netherlands scored a goal for each team and injured his own goalkeeper in the 1978 World Cup against Italy. The Dutch needed a win or a draw in the match to reach the final. Eighteen minutes into the game, Brandts kicked savagely at the ball in front of his own goal, knocked the ball into the netting, and crashed into Peter Schrijvers, the Netherlands goalkeeper. Schrijvers was carried off on a stretcher and replaced by Jan Jongbloed. Brandts recovered from the embarrassment by scoring on a free kick from 20 yards five minutes into the second half.

3. **RAJKO MITIC**

Yugoslavia's Rajko Mitic missed the start of the 1950 World Cup match against Brazil because he walked into a girder underneath Maracana Stadium in Rio de Janeiro on his way from the locker room to the field. Mitic received a severe cut on his forehead. At the time, substitutes weren't allowed, so the Yugoslavs had to decide whether to play at full strength without Mitic or start with ten men while Mitic was being stitched up. Yugoslavia started a man short, and Mitic joined the game later, but only after Brazil took a 1–0 lead en route to a 2–0 victory.

4. **RENE VAN DE KERKHOF**

Rene van de Kerkhof of the Netherlands injured his arm in the first game of the 1978 World Cup and in five subsequent matches played with a plastic cast protecting the injury. In the final against Argentina, the opposition complained to referee Sergio Gonella of Italy that the cast might be used as a weapon. The referee agreed, and the match was delayed for nine minutes while the cast was replaced with a soft bandage. Argentina went on to win 3–1.

5. **PATRICK BATTISON**

Patrick Battison was racing toward the West German goal in the 1982 World Cup semifinal when he was severely injured by West German goalkeeper Harald Schumacher. Schumacher smashed Battison to the ground, leaving the Frenchman unconscious for three minutes with injuries that sidelined him for six months. Despite the viciousness of the attack, Schumacher wasn't even given a yellow card. West Germany won on penalties after the two teams battled to a 3–3 tie.

6. DANIEL NIVEL

French police officer Daniel Nivel was left with permanent brain damage after he was clubbed over the head with a signpost by German hooligans in Lens during the 1998 World Cup. The 44-year-old Nivel was attacked while he was sitting in his police car.

7. RONNIE SIMPSON

The 1967 World Club Cup finals between Argentina's Racing Club and Scotland's Celtic was especially contentious, coming at a time when relations between Europe and South America were tense. The Cup was to be decided on goal aggregate with each club playing one home game. Celtic won the first match 1–0 in Glasgow. At the return match in Buenos Aires, Celtic goalkeeper Ronnie Simpson was struck by a rock thrown from the stands before the kickoff and couldn't play. Racing won 2–1. With the teams tied 2–2, a third match was scheduled at a neutral site in Montevideo, Uruguay. In the third match, Celtic had four players red carded and Racing two as the Argentine club won 1–0.

8. MEXICAN CHEERLEADERS

Four Mexican cheerleaders suffered burns on June 19, 1983, at the World Youth soccer championships at Azteca Stadium in Mexico City when Brazil won 1–0 over Argentina. The injuries were caused by balloons located under a net on the field which were ignited by sparks from fireworks detonated at the end of the match. The explosion threw flames onto the victims and caused third-degree burns.

9. GIANTS STADIUM MAINTENANCE WORKERS

The maintenance men at Giants Stadium in East Rutherford, New Jersey, fought with players from New York's Cosmos club during a practice session on July 6, 1979. Cosmos star Giorgio Chinglia tangled with the group, which was hired to clean up the stands, at the east end of the stadium after they called the player profane names and challenged him to a fight. Chinglia obliged and was joined by many of his teammates. Three of the maintenance workers were taken to the hospital after the melee. The trio filed charges against the Cosmos players, but they were cleared after a hearing.

10. U.S. TRAINER

The United States was blitzed by Argentina 6–1 in the 1930 World Cup semifinal in Montevideo, Uruguay, with an avalanche of five second-half goals. One American player after another had to be attended by the trainer because of vicious tackles by the Argentine players. The trainer was displeased when the referee gave a free kick to Argentina and dashed onto the field to protest. To emphasize his point, he threw his medical supplies to the ground, breaking a chloroform bottle. The fumes knocked the trainer out cold.

The Generals

No one knows the ups and downs of the game of soccer better than the coaches.

1. ADEMAR PIMENTA

Leonidas and Tim were two of Brazil's top players in 1938. Leonidas had scored six goals in the first two matches of the tournament, but Brazilian coach Ademar Pimenta left the two stars out of the lineup in the semifinal against Italy in Marseilles, France. Pimenta said he wanted Leonidas and Tim to be well-rested for the final. Brazil also brazenly booked the only available plane to Paris, where the final would be played, and made no provisions for travel to Bordeaux for the third-place match, which would be the team's destination should it lose. As it turned out, Leonidas and Tim were fresh for the final, but Brazil didn't play in the match because Italy beat them 2–1.

2. VICENTE FEOLA

Vicente Feola was the coach of Brazil's World Cup champions in 1958. Illness prevented him from directing the team in 1962 when the Brazilians won again, but Feola returned as coach in 1966. Playing in England, Brazil opened the 1966 tournament with a 2–0 win over Bulgaria but lost 3–1 to Hungary and 3–1 again against Portugal. There was so much outrage over the team's poor performance that Feola stayed in Europe for a month before sneaking back home.

3. **VITTORIO POZZO**

Italy's Vittorio Pozzo is the only individual to coach two teams that went all the way to the World Cup championship. He accomplished the feat in 1934 and 1938. The start of World War II prevented Pozzo from attempting a third straight title.

4. **PAULO MATA**

In Brazil in 1997, Itaperuna coach Paulo Mata was incensed that the referee allowed a late goal by the club Vasco de Gama to stand in the closing minute of a championship match in Rio de Janeiro. Already angry that his team had been issued three red cards for rough tackling, Mata protested that Edmundo was offside. The coach pulled off his shirt and rushed toward the referee. After being stopped by three policemen, Mata dropped his pants in full view of the television cameras and was led off the field still ranting at the officials. "I went naked," Mata explained, "because I'm tired of working honestly only to be scandalously robbed."

5. **DANIEL PASSARELLA**

Argentine national-team coach Daniel Passarella ordered that his players abstain from sex during the 1998 World Cup in France but later reversed his policy. He stated his athletes could have sex with their wives as long as it didn't take place in the team hotel. "There will be no objections if they rent a house or look for somewhere else to do it," said Passarella. "I believe it will be healthy."

6. **LORENZO SERRA FERRER**

Coach Lorenzo Serra Ferrer of Real Betis in Seville, Spain, reacted angrily to a parking ticket he received in 1996 from a police officer who was a season ticket holder of rival Sevilla. Serra Ferrer was charged with kicking the officer. Real Betis owner Manuel Ruiz de Lopera cried persecution, vowed to break up all relations with Seville City Hall, and blamed the officer for his club's 2–2 tie at home against underdog Racing Santander the following day. Serra Ferrer was dismissed as coach shortly thereafter, but he wasn't alone. In 1998, Ruiz de Lopera fired three coaches during the off-season.

7. **JOHN LAMBIE**

In 1992, during a training camp in the English seaside town of Blackpool, coach John Lambie of the Scottish First Division club Partick Thistle of Glasgow ended up in the hospital. Players decided to toss Lambie into the ocean as a prank, but he landed in 18 inches of water and suffered from fluid in his lungs and two broken ribs.

8. **JOCK STEIN**

Coach of Scotland's national team, Jock Stein died of a heart attack at the age of 62 on September 11, 1985, while Scotland played Wales to a 1–1 tie in a World Cup qualifying match in Cardiff. Stein coached Celtic to ten Scottish league titles, including nine in a row from 1966 through 1974.

9. **SEPP HERBERGER**

The coach of the 1954 West German World Cup team, Sepp Herberger, knew his squad would advance to the second round no matter what they did against Hungary in group play. Herberger intentionally fielded a weak lineup in order to rest his regulars. Hungary beat West Germany in an 8–3 runaway. Herberger's strategy worked when the two teams met again in the finals. A heavily favored and overconfident Hungary lost 3–2 to the West Germans.

10. **MARIO ZAGALO**

Mario Zagalo of Brazil is the only individual to play on two World Cup champions and coach another. He played left wing for Brazil's winning teams in 1958 and 1962 and scored a goal in each tournament. In 1970, he was named coach as a last-minute replacement for Joao Saldnha and led Brazil to another title. Zagalo is credited with stabilizing a Brazilian team wracked with dissension.

Animal Farm

A nimals have played a role in many of soccer's more bizarre incidents.

1. PICKLES

Scotland Yard sprang into action on March 20, 1966, when the Jules Rimet trophy, awarded to the World Cup champion, was stolen from Central Hall in Westminster Abbey in London. The trophy had been brought to England from Brazil to be displayed in advance of the World Cup in July. The trophy was discovered a few days later by a mongrel dog named Pickles. The canine was digging for a bone in the backyard of his owner's London home and instead unearthed the memento. Police tracked the crime to Edward Betchley, who stole the trophy to hold it for ransom. Pickles became a national hero.

2. BUTTERFLIES

During a World Cup qualifying match between Cameroon and Guinea in Yaounde, Cameroon, millions of black butterflies invaded the stadium. The contest went on amid the swirling butterflies, and Cameroon won 3–1.

3. PIGEONS

The Spanish club Atletico Madrid has a severe pigeon problem at its home of Estadio Vicente Calderon. The birds peck at the grass, creating large areas of nothing but dirt. The club tried leaving pigeon carcasses on the field and brought cats into the stadium, but the efforts were in vain.

4. CANARY ISLANDS

In 1995, a vulture with a wingspan of more than six feet escaped from a bird sanctuary in the Canary Islands and flew to a neighboring soccer field in Tenerife. The bird attacked the referee and several players who tried to get it off the field. Fortunately, there were no serious injuries and no reports of canaries attacking players in the Vulture Islands.

5. BRAZIL

In 1995, Brazil's soccer fans were warned they would be arrested if they were caught carrying animals into stadiums. The warning came after a Flamengo–Vasco de Gama match in the Rio de Janeiro championship during which dozens of Flamengo fans brought animals to the stadium in tribute to Edmundo, who is also nicknamed "The Animal." Most of the animals were dogs dressed in Flamengo shirts and hats. One man was seen waving a tortoise with a Flamengo flag painted on its shell. "The place for native fauna is in the wild," said Pedro Cavalieri, an official with the Brazilian government's environmental agency.

6. SAUDI ARABIA

In 1990, Saudi Arabia refused to play in the annual Gulf Cup tournament set in Kuwait. The Saudis were upset by Kuwait's choice of logo: two horses symbolizing a 1919 battle in which Kuwaiti tribes had defeated Saudi attackers.

7. JONATHAN LIVINGSTON SEAGULL

In 1999, a seagull scored a goal during an English youth-league match. Danny Worthington, a 13-year-old striker with the Stalybridge Celtic Colts, volleyed from 25 yards and turned away because he thought he had missed. Suddenly, a seagull swooped down, and the ball glanced off the bird's head and into the goal. The referee allowed the score to stand. The stunned bird plunged to earth but recovered and flew away.

8. A WHITE HORSE

The first match held at Wembley Stadium in London took place on April 28, 1923, an English FA Cup final between Bolton and West Ham United. Nobody anticipated such a large turnout. The stadium was filled to its 125,000 capacity, a crowd which included King George V. An estimated 250,000 tried to gain admittance, and many thousands forced their way in and flooded the field, making play impossible. Police led by Constable George Scorey on his legendary white horse, Billy, cleared the field. The match began an hour late. The first goal was scored by Bolton's David Jack and came as a West Ham defender was trying to climb back out of the crowd next to the touchline. Bolton's second goal, which sealed a 2–0 victory, bounced off spectators standing on the goal netting.

9. A BLACKBIRD

In the 1938 World Cup semifinal against Hungary in Paris, Sweden pounced quickly by scoring just 35 seconds into the match on a goal by Arne Nyberg. The rest of the contest was no contest, as Hungary routed the Swedes, playing on the 80th birthday of their monarch King Gustav, by a count of 5–1. Play was so concentrated in the Swedish half of the field that a blackbird alighted on the Hungarian half and leisurely pecked at the grass for several minutes completely undisturbed.

10. **A BRAZILIAN COW**

During the 1982 World Cup, a farmer in the state of Amazonas inadvertently asphyxiated his cow by painting the Brazilian flag across its flanks.

Celebration!

Celebrations of victories and goals by players and fans have manifested themselves in strange ways.

1. JUAN HOHBERG

Juan Hohberg of Uruguay scored a goal with four minutes remaining in regulation to tie Hungary 2–2 in the semifinals of the 1954 World Cup in Lausanne, Switzerland, but was knocked out cold when his teammates rushed en masse to celebrate. Hohberg recovered and hit the post with a shot in extra time, but Uruguay lost 4–2.

2. ROBBIE FOWLER

Liverpool's Robbie Fowler celebrated a goal in a 1999 match against Everton by pretending to snort the endline after fans heckled him with insinuations of drug use. Fowler was suspended four games and fined $52,000 by the English FA. Earlier in the season, he had been suspended two games for making a homophobic gesture toward another player.

3. **BRIANA SCURRY**

After the United States women won the championship match at the 1996 Atlanta Olympics, American goalkeeper Briana Scurry ran along a secluded street of Athens, Georgia, wearing her gold medal—and nothing else.

4. **FINIDI GEORGE**

In the 1994 World Cup, Finidi George of Nigeria crawled to a corner after scoring a goal against Greece, lifted a leg, and pretended to use the corner flag as a dog would use a fire hydrant. Several of George's teammates followed in the ritual.

5. **CELESTINE BABAYARO**

Celestine Babayaro of England's Chelsea club twice injured himself in 1993 by doing back flips after scoring a goal. Management threatened huge fines if he did it again.

6. **LES SHARPE**

During the early 1990s, Les Sharpe of Manchester United liked to uproot a corner flag after scoring a goal and hold it like a microphone while performing an impersonation of Elvis Presley.

7. **IXIAMAS, BOLIVIA**

Fans in Ixiamas, Bolivia, were so excited by their country's 3–1 win over Uruguay in a World Cup qualifying match on August 9, 1993, that they allowed their village to burn to the ground. Amid the celebrations, residents failed to notice that 40 houses, which comprised most of the village, were on fire. By the time they did notice, it was too late to save any of the homes, and all were destroyed. The blaze was caused by firecrackers which fell on the palm-leaf thatched roofs during celebrations.

8. WOLFIE

Wolfie, the mascot of England's Wolverhampton club, did a little too much celebrating over his team's victory on November 7, 1998. During a First Division match between home team Bristol City and Wolverhampton at Ashton Gate, the battle between the mascots was more entertaining than the game. Wolverhampton built a 6–1 lead, and Wolfie began taunting Bristol City's mascot, City Cat, and three pig mascots representing a Bristol double-glazing company. The three little pigs had enough and attacked the big, bad Wolfie, throwing a series of punches. City Cat soon joined in the fray and added a few well-placed right crosses. Unamused by the fracas, which resembled an odd melding of a nursery fable and a Monty Python sketch, a Bristol City official said, "City Cat has been sacked."

9. SIR HAROLD THOMPSON

In 1980, Sir Harold Thompson, chairman of England's FA, said that players should cease kissing, hugging, and jumping on the backs of teammates after a goal is scored. Thompson suggested that all a player needed to do was to place his arm around a teammate's shoulder and say "well done."

10. BRANDI CHASTAIN

After winning the 1999 women's World Cup for the United States against China with a penalty kick, Brandi Chastain fell to her knees, whipped off her jersey, and waved it above her head. Regulation play had ended in a scoreless tie at the

Rose Bowl in Pasadena, California. Chastain broke a 4–4 tie in the penalty phase with a laser past Chinese goalkeeper Gao Hong. In 1991, when the U.S. won the first women's World Cup, the accomplishment barely registered on the national consciousness. The 1999 victory made the U.S. women's soccer team a national conversation piece. The championship match was witnessed by 40 million on U.S. television.

Are You Blind?

Soccer has fewer playing rules than any major sport, but the referee has more responsibility and can affect the outcome of a contest in more ways than an official in just about any other type of competition.

1. JEAN LANGENUS

Jean Langenus of Belgium refereed the first World Cup final between Uruguay and Argentina on July 30, 1930, in Montevideo, Uruguay. A controversy erupted because each team wanted to use its own ball. Langenus decreed that each ball would be used for one half. Argentina won the toss and elected to use its ball for the first half. Uruguay scored first, but Argentina took a 2–1 lead by halftime. Uruguay had its ball in the second half and scored three times for a 4–2 victory.

2. ALMEIDA REGO

Almeida Rego of Brazil was the referee for the match between Argentina and France during the 1930 World Cup. Argentina led 1–0 with six minutes left in the match when Marcel Langiller of France raced the length of the field with the ball. As he closed in on the goal, Rego blew his whistle to signal time had expired. The French protested, and Rego realized he had called the contest too early. After play resumed, the dispirited French players failed to score, and Argentina came away with a controversial 1–0 decision.

3. CLIVE THOMAS

With the score 1–1 between Brazil and Sweden in the 1978 World Cup at Mar del Plata, Argentina, Zico of Brazil headed in an apparent goal, but referee Clive Thomas of Wales blew his whistle for time a split second before the ball crossed the goal line. Brazil protested vehemently, but the score remained 1–1.

4. TRINIDAD

Trinidad and Haiti met in a World Cup qualifying match in Port-au-Prince, Haiti, on December 4, 1973. A victory for either team would have qualified it for the World Cup for the first time. Trinidad had four goals disallowed by a Salvadoran referee, however, and lost 2–1. Haiti hasn't qualified for the World Cup since, while Trinidad (now Trinidad and Tobago) is still looking for its first opportunity to compete in the final rounds.

5. ABRAHAM KLEIN

Abraham Klein of Israel was the first choice to referee the 1978 World Cup final between Argentina and the Netherlands but was replaced by Sergio Gonella of Italy when Argentine officials complained because of the Netherlands' close political ties to Israel.

6. ANTONIO MANARI

During a Serie C match in Italy between Castel San Pietro and home team Rimini on April 27, 1998, which ended in a 1–1 draw, the crowd was so angered over the calls of referee Antonio Manari that he had to flee in a helicopter provided by the police.

7. MARCELLO CARDONA

Referee Marcello Cardona of Italy suspended a match with Salernitana leading Foggia 3–1 in the 89th minute because fans invaded the field. Since the match didn't come to a conclusion, it wasn't included in Italy's National Olympic Committee lottery in which fans predict the result of matches to win cash. The referee's decision cost one bettor 12 billion lire ($7.6 million).

8. JANET FREWINGS

Women are permitted to referee men's games in England, but many soccer fans believe that 41-year-old Janet Frewings overstepped her bounds. In 1996, she was charged with bringing the game into disrepute for stripping off to shower with the players after matches. "We are aware that changing facilities are far from ideal," said an English FA official. "However, we believe the referees or their assistants should make their own arrangements."

9. HUSSAIN KANDIL

During a 1970 World Cup match between Mexico and El Salvador, Egyptian referee Hussain Kandil awarded El Salvador a free kick with the contest still scoreless late in the first half. Due to the referee's error, however, the kick was quickly taken by a Mexican player and went for a score. Kandil allowed the goal to stand instead of disallowing it, returning the ball to the previous spot, and allowing El Salvador to take possession. El Salvador argued for four minutes and nearly walked off the field in protest. Two players received yellow cards for venting their objections too strongly. Mexico easily defeated the disheartened Salvadoran team 4–0.

10. **ARGENTINA**

A 1992 match between Regional and Estudiantes in Argentina was headed for a tie when it was interrupted by four parachutists who were blown off course and landed in the middle of the field. Startled by the sight, an Estudiantes player picked up the game ball. Unfortunately, he was standing in the penalty area, and the referee awarded a penalty kick which gave Regional the victory. "Even if they were flying saucers," said the unsympathetic official, "a handball in the area is a penalty."

Celebrities

Many of the world's great celebrities have been connected with soccer in some manner.

1. POPE JOHN PAUL II

Born Karol Wojtyla, Pope John Paul II was a goalie during his youth for the State Secondary School for Boys in Wadowice, Poland. The Cracovia club in Krakow, Poland, has been the Pope's beloved team since his boyhood. The club won Poland's championship in 1921, 1930, 1932, 1937, and 1948.

2. ARNOLD SCHWARZENEGER

Hollywood star Arnold Schwarzeneger helped finance the building of a new stadium in his hometown of Graz, Austria. The city of Graz has supplanted Vienna to become a new power base for Austrian soccer with its two clubs, Sturm and Grazer AK.

3. PRINCE ALBERT OF MONACO

The most famous supporter of AS Monaco, which won the championship of France for the seventh time in 2000, is Prince Albert of Monaco. Another fan of AS Monaco is Boris

Becker, who lives in the cliff-top principality to escape the high taxes of his native Germany.

4. FRANCO ZEFFERELLI

Film director Franco Zefferelli, an avid fan of the Fiorentina club in Italy, publicly suggested that rival Juventus had bribed referees to win its final game of the season against Roma and edge out Fiorentina for the Serie A title in 1982. Juventus sued Zefferelli, and the court ordered him to pay the team $30,000 in damages.

5. DAVID BECKHAM

England's soccer sensation David Beckham married Spice Girl Victoria Adams, also known as Posh Spice, in 1998. Beckham saw Adams in a video on TV and was determined to meet her. They met after a Manchester United match in March 1997.

6. HENRY KISSINGER

A former U.S. secretary of state under Richard Nixon and Gerald Ford, Henry Kissinger grew up playing soccer in his native Germany and is a huge fan. He attended the World Cup in both 1974 in West Germany and in 1978 in Argentina. Kissinger also led an unsuccessful bid to convince the FIFA to allow the United States to host soccer's premier event in 1986.

7. STEPHEN REA

Before leaving for Yugoslavia to make the film *Citizen X* in 1994, Irish actor Stephen Rea made certain his contract gave him time off to travel to the United States in order to see Ireland play in the World Cup.

8. **ELTON JOHN**

Pop star Elton John bought controlling interest in the Watford club in England in 1972. He wasn't just a figurehead but a successful owner who helped bring Watford from the Fourth Division in 1977–78 to the top flight for the first time in club history in 1982. John eventually lost his enthusiasm, however, and by 1990 he took a backseat in the club's operations. Watford again dropped to the bottom of the standings and was relegated to a lower division. In 1995, John returned, and Watford again rose to the Premier League. He also owned a piece of the Los Angeles Aztecs in the North American Soccer League during the 1970s. The Philadelphia Fury of the NASL boasted celebrity owners Mick Jagger, Paul Simon, and Peter Frampton.

9. **SEAN CONNERY**

As a teenager, Sean Connery played professional soccer in his native Scotland for Bonnyrig Rose Athletic.

10. **SYLVESTER STALLONE**

In between making *Rocky 2* and *Rocky 3,* Stallone starred in a soccer movie called *Victory* in 1981. Stallone played an American in a World War II German POW camp with an international cast that included Michael Caine and soccer stars Pele and Bobby Moore. Stallone's character had never played soccer before but was made goalkeeper for the prisoner's soccer team because he was once a top baseball player and could catch a ball better than anyone else in the camp. The prisoners accepted a challenge to play a match against their captors and, after winning the contest, escaped through the sewers of Paris.

Last Line of Defense

Goalkeeping is a club's last line of defense, and it takes a unique individual to handle the demands of the position.

1. DOK-YUNG HONG

South Korea's Dok-yung Hong is the only goalkeeper to allow 16 scores in consecutive matches in the World Cup final rounds. In 1954, South Korea fell to Hungary 9–0 on June 17 in Zurich, Switzerland, and 7–0 versus Turkey three days later in Geneva.

2. ALEX THEPOT

In the first World Cup match in history, July 13, 1930, French goalkeeper Alex Thepot was kicked in the jaw and suffered a concussion just 10 minutes into the match against Mexico, necessitating his removal from the field. Since no substitutions were allowed at the time, France had to make do with 10 players and a halfback in goal for the rest of the match. France still managed to win 4–1. Thepot returned for France's two remaining games in the tournament, but the French lost 1–0 to Argentina and 1–0 to Chile.

3. **VALENTIN BARGAN**

Romanian goalkeeper Valentin Bargan left the Recolta Laza club in 1998 to sign with rival Stemmic Buda. He was lured away by a doubling of his salary, but Bargan said the clincher was that his new team threw in a truckload of logs for his wood-heated home.

4. **JEAN-MARIE PFAFF**

Shortly before a match against El Salvador in the World Cup on June 19, 1982, in Eiche, Spain, Belgian goalkeeper Jean-Marie Pfaff nearly drowned in an accident at the team's hotel. Pfaff recovered sufficiently to help Belgium shut down El Salvador and win 1–0.

5. **MOACIR BARBOSA**

Moacir Barbosa of Brazil gave up the goal which allowed Uruguay to win the 1950 World Cup by a 2–1 score. He was hounded and mocked mercilessly for the rest of his life. Barbosa died virtually penniless at the age of 79 in 2000. In 1993, he went to the Brazilian training camp to offer encouragement to the team during World Cup qualifying but was denied admission for fear he would bring the team bad luck.

6. **OLAV FISKE**

In 2000, during a Norwegian Cup amateur match, Surnadal goalkeeper Olav Fiske relieved himself behind the net during the break between the two overtime periods. The referee signaled for the kickoff more quickly than Fiske anticipated, and Sunndal striker Oddvar Torve spotted the open net and scored to give his team a 1–0 win. Fiske was quite literally caught with his pants down.

7. **WALTER ZENGA**

Playing for Italy in 1990, Walter Zenga set the record for the most consecutive minutes in World Cup play without surrendering a goal, a span of 517 minutes. He was unscored upon in the first five games of the tournament and wasn't beaten until the 67th minute of the semifinal against Argentina in Naples. The match ended in a 1−1 tie before Argentina won 4−3 on penalties. Zenga beat the old record of 499 minutes set by Peter Shilton of England in 1982 and 1986. Zenga and Shilton squared off in goal in the third-place playoff in 1990, which the Italians won 2−1.

8. **ANTONIO CARBAJAL**

Mexico's goalkeeper Antonio Carbajal has played in five World Cup final rounds, more than any player in history. Carbajal appeared in matches in 1950, 1954, 1958, 1962, and 1966.

9. **GORDON BANKS**

Gordon Banks of England was the world's top goalkeeper when he injured his eyes in a car accident in 1972 and was forced to retire. His twisting save on a Pele header in the World Cup in 1970 is recognized as the greatest ever in the history of the tournament.

10. **SAMOA**

October 9, 1998, was a bad day for goalkeepers from Samoa. In qualifying for the women's World Cup, Australia clobbered Western Samoa 21−0 and New Zealand routed American Samoa by the same 21−0 score.

International Incidents

I nternational soccer competition has caused, or been a party to, many international incidents, including war.

1. THE "SOCCER WAR"

Honduras and El Salvador met in a three-match qualifying series in 1969 to decide which nation would advance to the final rounds of the 1970 World Cup at a time when the governments of the two nations had been involved in long-smoldering and deep-seated disputes over social and economic issues. Each side won on its home soil. A playoff was held in Mexico City on June 28, and El Salvador won 3–2 in extra time. Each of the three matches saw clashes between the fans of the two nations. After the third match, diplomatic relations between Honduras and El Salvador were severed, and on July 14, a four-day war broke out along the border. The death toll was in excess of 10,000 people, most of them civilians, with many more thousands left homeless.

2. KOSOVO

In 1991, FK Pristina of Kosovo was driven from its stadium and kicked out of the Yugoslavian League by Serbian police as part of the authorities' crackdown on ethnic Albanians in the city. FK Pristina returned on July 22, 1999, to play a team from Tetova, Macedonia, in the shadow of a police station that had been gutted by a NATO missile.

3. WILLI LEMKE

A player and coach in Germany, Willi Lemke was a double agent for West Germany and the Soviet KGB for five years during the 1970s. In a 1995 interview, Lemke said he became a spy out of a "yearning for adventure, vanity, curiosity, and a duty to my country." The adventure began at the age of 24 when Lemke was approached by the Soviet vice-consul in East Germany and asked to work for the KGB. The Soviets believed Lemke could lead them to left-leaning students like himself. Lemke informed the West German intelligence agency, however, and kept them appraised of KGB activities in East Germany.

4. ENGLAND AND GERMANY

England met Germany in a friendly international match on May 14, 1938, at Olympic Stadium in Berlin. In an effort to placate and appease Adolf Hitler, England forced its team to give the Nazi salute as the German national anthem was being played. The instruction came from British Ambassador to Germany Sir Neville Henderson and was supported by the English FA. The players reluctantly gave the salute, then pounded the Germans 6–3. Prior to a match against Italy in Milan on May 18, 1939, which ended in a 2–2 draw, the English players gave the Fascist salute to all four corners of the field. By September 1939, England was at war with both Germany and Italy.

5. **HITLER'S BIRTHDAY**

On April 6, 1994, England pulled out of a match against Germany in Berlin scheduled for April 20—Adolf Hitler's birthday—because of fears of violence. England's FA cited evidence that both pro- and anti-Nazi demonstrations were planning to converge on Berlin the day of the game. Furthermore, the match was scheduled for Olympic Stadium in Berlin, the site of Hitler's propaganda exercise at the 1936 Olympic games.

6. **GABON AND THE CONGO**

In 1962, Gabon expelled 3,000 Congolese residents because of bitterness that grew out of a soccer match played during the African Nations' Cup. Gabon had defeated the Congo 3–1 in Libreville, Gabon's capital. A return match was slated for Brazzaville, the Congo's capital city. The Congo won 3–1, but Congolese fans thought the referee deprived them of at least two goals. Gabon Premier Leon Mba said that the Congo fans displayed bad sportsmanship and issued the order to expel all of Congolese in Gabon after irate Gabonese burned homes and beat up Congolese immigrants, leaving nine dead. In retaliation, Gabonese immigrants in the Congo were attacked, with at least one death.

7. **THE FIRST WORLD CUP FINAL**

Neighbors Argentina and Uruguay met in the first World Cup final, played on July 30, 1930, in Montevideo. Thousands of Argentine supporters crossed the River Plate, which separated the two countries, by the boatload. After Uruguay won 4–2, Argentine fans expressed their anger by throwing bricks through the windows of the Uruguayan embassy in Buenos Aires.

8. THE 1936 OLYMPICS

Peru and Austria met in the quarterfinals of the 1936 Olympics. During the second overtime period with the score tied 2–2, Peruvian fans rushed onto the field and attacked one of the Austrian players. Peru scored twice to win 4–2, but as a result of the assault on the Austrian player, the International Olympic Committee ordered that the game be replayed two days later behind locked doors with no spectators allowed. Peru refused to show up, and the entire Peruvian Olympic team withdrew in protest. Colombia also withdrew in support of its South American neighbor. Peru's President Oscar Benavides publicly denounced the decision, and demonstrators threw rocks at the Austrian consulate in Lima.

9. WEST AND EAST GERMANY

East Germany reached the final rounds of the World Cup only once, and it seemed fitting that the East Germans should meet the West Germans. It happened in the third match of first-round group play on June 22, 1974, in Hamburg. Security was tight, but the only shocking activity was on the field, where East Germany pulled off a 1–0 upset on a goal by Jurgen Sparwasser with 10 minutes remaining in regulation. After the defeat, West Germany won four in a row to clinch the championship. It was the only win for East Germany, which also lost twice and played to a draw.

10. THE ENGLISH IN MEXICO

England won the World Cup in 1966 but had few friends in Latin America. Throughout the 1960s, European teams, particularly those from England and Scotland, had played several brutal matches against clubs from South and Central

America. The rivalry peaked at the 1970 World Cup in Mexico. Before their second match against Brazil, the English players were "serenaded" at 3 A.M. by a couple hundred Mexicans, most of them equipped with drums, frying pans, horns, and other noisemakers. England reached the quarter-finals before losing 3–2 to West Germany.

Behind the Iron Curtain

It has been nearly impossible to separate politics from soccer in the Soviet Union, present-day Russia, and other Eastern European nations.

1. SOCCER FIELDS IN CUBA

It was the presence of soccer fields in Cuba that tipped off the United States that the Soviet Union was secretly building a submarine base at Cienfuegos, Cuba, during the Nixon administration. The discovery was made by satellite photos. The base violated an understanding reached in 1962 following the Cuban missile crisis. Soccer fan Henry Kissinger knew immediately the significance of the soccer fields. "Cubans play baseball," said Kissinger. "Russians play soccer."

2. 1968 EUROPEAN CUP

The Soviet Union withdrew from the European Cup tournament in 1968 in protest of the realignment of matches following the Soviet intervention in Czechoslovakia. The Soviets had sent troops into Czechoslovakia to quell an uprising for

Czech self-determination. The Soviets were joined in the boy-cott by allies Poland, Hungary, Bulgaria, and East Germany. The action followed a decision by the European Football Union to revise first-round matches to keep apart teams from Eastern and Western Europe to "avoid possible boy-cotts of certain clubs following the military and political events in Czechoslovakia."

3. OLYMPICS

With the lines between professionalism and amateurism blurred beyond recognition behind the Iron Curtain, commu-nist countries dominated the Olympic soccer competition from 1952 through 1988. They won the gold medal in every Olympic competition during those years except 1984, when communist nations boycotted the Olympics in Los Angeles. Winners of the gold were Hungary (1952, 1964, and 1968), the Soviet Union (1956 and 1988), Yugoslavia (1960), Poland (1972), East Germany (1976), and Czechoslovakia (1980).

4. WORLD CUP

Eastern European countries haven't been as successful in the World Cup, failing to win a single championship. When Germany was divided at the end of World War II, it was capi-talist West Germany that became one of the top soccer nations in the world while communist East Germany reached the final rounds only once. The Soviet Union/Russia holds the record, in a tie with Yugoslavia, for most victories in World Cup competition without winning a championship. In fact, the nation's best finish was fourth place in 1966. The Soviet/ Russian record in the World Cup is 16-12-6. The records of other Iron Curtain countries are: Yugoslavia 16-13-8, Hungary

15-14-3, Poland 13-7-5, Czechoslovakia (now Czech Republic) 11-14-5, and Romania 8-8-5.

5. MOSCOW DYNAMO

Shortly after the close of World War II, the Moscow Dynamo toured Great Britain in November 1945 and failed to lose a match. The Dynamo overwhelmed Cardiff City 10−1 in Wales, defeated Arsenal 4−3 in a thick fog, and tied Chelsea 3−3 and the Rangers 2−2 in Glasgow.

6. LUZHNIKI DISASTER

In 1982, Spartak Moscow played Haarlem of the Netherlands in a UEFA Cup match at Luzhniki Stadium in Moscow. As fans were climbing the icy steps to leave, a last-minute Spartak goal was scored. Fans tried to return to their seats, and an awful crush occurred in which more than 300 people lost their lives. The enormity of the disaster was kept a secret from the Soviet people for seven years.

7. 1952 OLYMPICS

During the second round at the 1952 Olympics in Helsinki, Finland, the Soviet Union soccer team competed for the first time and trailed Yugoslavia 5−1 before rallying with four goals to tie 5−5. The contest was replayed, and Yugoslavia won 3−1. The defeat wasn't mentioned in the Soviet press until after the death of Joseph Stalin a year later.

8. POLES IN SPAIN

More than 300 Poles who came to watch the 1982 World Cup in Spain defected and sought asylum in the West. "This is our only chance," said one. "We have nothing to expect from life in Poland." Poland had been under martial law since December 1981. Polish police had carefully screened fans who were allowed to attend the event, believing they would return. The soccer fans were permitted to take only $60 out of the country.

q. **ALEXANDER BRAGIN**

On October 16, 1995, a bomb exploded at the start of a match in Donetsk, Ukraine, killing Alexander Bragin, the president of Shakhtar Donetsk, and five other people. Four of the victims were bodyguards hired to protect him. The match against Tavria Simferopol, before a crowd of 8,000, was called off. Bragin was a controversial figure in Donetsk, a grim coal-mining city of more than one million. Bragin had survived three previous attempts on his life over the previous 18 months.

10. **OLEG VERETENNIKOV**

Russian star Oleg Veretennikov, who played for Rotor Volgograd, was attacked in 1998 by an unknown assailant who poured acid on him while he was walking with his two-year-old daughter. The little girl was placed in critical condition with burns on her hands.

Murder and Death

The murder and death of individuals has been an all too frequent occurrence in the annals of soccer.

1. JOE GAETJENS

Joe Gaetjens scored the goal for the United States that upset England 1–0 in the 1950 World Cup. Gaetjens was a native of Haiti who was never a naturalized U.S. citizen but was eligible for the U.S. World Cup team because he had applied for citizenship. At the time, he was working as a dishwasher in New York City while taking accounting courses. Gaetjens later played professionally in France before returning to Haiti. Around 1970, he was arrested by the government of Haitian president Francois Duvalier and was never seen again.

2. ANDRES ESCOBAR

Many experts believed that Colombia would win the World Cup in 1994, but the team didn't even reach the second round, in part because of a 2–1 loss on June 22 to the United States at the Rose Bowl. During the U.S. match, Colombia's Andres

Escobar accidentally sent a ball into his own net as he attempted to clear a pass by John Harkes. The goal gave the United States a 1–0 lead. When he returned to Colombia, Escobar was shot 12 times as he left a nightclub near Medelin. One of the gunmen shouted, "Goal, Goal."

3. ALEX VILLAPLANE

Alex Villaplane was the captain of the French side during the first World Cup match played in 1930. In 1944, after the liberation of France from the Nazis, Villaplane was executed by a firing squad for collaborating with the Germans.

4. SALAH ASSAD

Instrumental in leading Algeria to a 2–1 upset of West Germany during the 1982 World Cup, Salah Assad was arrested and executed in 1992 during an Algerian government-ordered crackdown on Islamic fundamentalists in the country.

5. SAM OKWARJI

One of Nigeria's top players, 24-year-old Sam Okwarji collapsed and died of a heart attack during a World Cup qualifying match against Angola on August 13, 1989. Okwarji had just signed a $500,000 contract to play for a club in Belgium. There were ten minutes left in Nigeria's 1–0 victory in Lagos when Okwarji collapsed. Okwarji's death wasn't the only tragedy during the match. Seven fans also died of suffocation because 100,000 had crowded into a stadium designed to hold 80,000. Okwarji and the seven fans may have been saved, but the key to the locker containing the CPR equipment couldn't be found.

6. **PERU**

A spectator at a soccer match in Peru fatally shot an opposing player who had just scored a goal. Maximo Ayala, a fan of Deportivo Rayo, killed Rafael Palomino of Deportivo Atlas with a shotgun and injured four others during the match at Cabriza in the Peruvian Andes. Ayala was angry because his team was losing 3–0 in the closing minutes. He had bet heavily on Deportivo Rayo to win.

7. **TURKEY**

After the Turkish club Galatasaray defeated England's Leeds United on April 6, 2000, fans in Istanbul celebrated by firing shots into the air. One man was killed when a ricocheting bullet struck him in the head.

8. **BILL LEE**

Bill Lee, a 17-year-old apprentice with the Burnley club in England, was killed on March 10, 1992, when he fell through the roof of Turf Moor Stadium while retrieving a ball. A club official said Lee was carrying out his normal duties when he spotted the ball, and that the youngster ignored warning signs to stay off the roof.

9. **SWEDEN**

A woman in Sweden was charged with murder for killing her boyfriend with a pair of scissors after he forced her to stay up and watch the early morning telecast of the Sweden-Cameroon match during the 1994 World Cup. She had fallen asleep, and her boyfriend woke her and told her not to go back to sleep. An argument ensued, and the woman stabbed him to death. "I'd had enough," she explained to police. After committing the murder, she went back to sleep. Friends discovered her in a sound, peaceful sleep next to the dead body.

10. **DOMINIQUE RUTILY**

Dominique Rutily, the president of France's Fifth Division National 3 club on Corsica, was murdered in 1996 following his team's match against Hyeres. Rutily was shot four times in the head at close range as he was getting into his car. Rutily was apparently the victim of a gangland feud. He had been under investigation several years earlier in connection with an armed robbery but was never charged.

Notorious Matches

Several matches through the years have exhibited the seamier side of the sport.

1. WEST GERMANY VS. AUSTRIA, 1982

West Germany and Austria met in group play in the 1982 World Cup in Spain. West Germany needed a win to advance to the second round, while Austria could advance if it lost by fewer than three goals. If either team failed, Algeria would advance. West Germany scored in the 11th minute, and since a 1–0 score guaranteed both teams' entry into the second round, they proceeded to maneuver the ball around the middle of the field without attempting to score. One West German fan was so disgusted that he set fire to his national flag on the terraces. Algerian fans in the stands cried fix and jeered the teams. Neither West Germany nor Austria was penalized after an investigation by the FIFA.

2. ARGENTINA VS. PERU, 1978

Argentina took the field against Peru in the 1978 World Cup needing not just a win to reach the World Cup final, but a win with at least four goals and with a margin of at least three scores. If Argentina failed, Brazil would advance to play the Netherlands for the championship. Argentina won 6–0, causing the Brazilians to unsuccessfully level allegations of a fix. Peru's goalkeeper was Ramon Quiroga, who was born in Argentina but acquired Peruvian citizenship and became eligible for that country's national team.

3. HUNGARY VS. BRAZIL, 1954

In what has become known as the notorious "Battle of Berne," Hungary and Brazil played a match in the quarterfinals of the 1954 World Cup in a pelting rain on June 27 in Berne, Switzerland. Hungary went ahead 2–0 after eight minutes and held on to win 4–2. The two teams spent as much time kicking each other as they did booting the ball. After the match, the Brazilians hid in the tunnel leading to the locker rooms and waited for the Hungarians. The teams fought for 20 minutes, using broken bottles as weapons according to some reports, and sustained several casualties. During Hungary's next match against Uruguay, Swiss officials surrounded the field with troops, but there were no further incidents as Hungary won 4–2.

4. ENGLAND VS. ARGENTINA, 1966

England and Argentina met at Wembley Stadium in London in a bruising quarterfinal match in the 1966 World Cup that kept West German referee Rudolf Kreitlein busy. Nine minutes from halftime, he ejected Argentina's Antonio Rattin for "violence of the tongue." Rattin refused to leave the field for eight minutes. England scored in the second half on a header by Geoff Hurst in the 78th minute and held on to win 1–0. At the end of the game, Argentina's players began pummeling

Kreitlein, who was rescued by police. England's coach, Alf Ramsey, refused to let his players exchange shirts with the Argentines, whom he described as "animals." Ramsey apologized, but the comment escalated animosities among teams from Europe and South America and would hinder international relations between the two continents for years.

5. CHILE VS. ITALY, 1962

An Italian journalist stirred things up before host Chile and Italy met in Santiago during the 1962 World Cup by penning an article that criticized living conditions in Chile. The Chilean team was bent on revenge. Italy's Giorgio Ferrini was ejected only eight minutes into the match. Ferrini refused to leave the field for 10 minutes and then did so only because he was escorted by police. Five minutes prior to halftime, Leonel Sanchez of Chile punched Italy's Humberto Maschio with a left hook that was clearly seen by a worldwide television audience and everyone in the stadium. Everyone, that is, except referee Ken Aston of England and the two linesmen, who refused to eject Sanchez. Later, Sanchez set up Chile's first goal in the 74th minute, and Chile won the match 2–0.

6. CZECHOSLOVAKIA VS. BRAZIL, 1938

The match between Czechoslovakia and Brazil in the 1938 World Cup in Bordeaux, France, is one of the most vicious international matches on record. Three players were ejected, and three Czechs suffered devastating injuries. The match ended in a 1–1 tie. Two days later, the two teams met in the replay, but 15 of the 22 players who participated in the previous meeting were unable to compete because of injuries. Brazil won the replay 2–1 in a cleanly played match.

7. **WEST GERMANY VS. ARGENTINA, 1990**

The worst-played final in World Cup history is the one which pitted West Germany against Argentina in Rome in 1990. The Argentine players seemed more interested in injuring their opponents and complaining to the referee than in playing soccer. West Germany won 1–0 on a penalty kick by Andreas Brehme in the 84th minute.

8. **ARGENTINA VS. CHILE, 1930**

During the first half of Argentina's 3–1 win over Chile in the 1930 World Cup in Montevideo, Uruguay, police had to be called onto the field to quell a brawl between the players.

9. **INDONESIA VS. THAILAND, 1998**

Both Indonesia and Thailand had already qualified for the semifinals of the Tiger Cup in Ho Chi Minh City, Vietnam, when they met in group play on August 31, 1998. The winner was to play Vietnam, while the loser was slated to face Singapore. Vietnam was considered to be a much stronger opponent than Singapore, however, and both Indonesia and Thailand played 90 minutes trying to lose. With seconds left in regulation, Indonesia's Mursyid Effendi kicked a ball into his own goal to give Thailand a 3–2 win. Fortunately, Indonesia wasn't rewarded for the loss, losing to Singapore in the semifinals 2–1.

10. **NORTHERN IRELAND VS. ITALY, 1958**

In World Cup qualifying, Northern Ireland needed a victory and Italy a tie to advance to the World Cup final rounds in Sweden in 1958. A match was scheduled in Belfast to decide the issue, but Hungarian referee Istvan Zsolt was stranded by fog at the London airport and couldn't arrive in time. The Italians refused a substitute for Zsolt, and the two nations agreed to play a "friendly." There was nothing friendly about the match, however, as the Italians seemed bent on injuring as many players from Northern Ireland as possible. The contest ended in a 2–2 tie. A month later, Italy and Northern Ireland met again, with Zsolt as the referee, and Northern Ireland won 2–1. It's one of only two times that Italy failed to play in the World Cup final rounds. The other was in 1930 when Italy refused to travel to Uruguay for the event.

Protesting Too Much

Things don't always go as players and fans think they should, leading to inevitable protests.

1. **PORTUGAL'S 1986 WORLD CUP TEAM**

Angered by the refusal of team officials to double their bonuses, Portugal's 1986 World Cup players decided to go on strike and boycott training sessions through the start of the tournament. Portugal's President Mario Soares sent a telegram appealing to officials and players to resolve their differences. One day later, the players abandoned their boycott. Once play began, Portugal surprised England with a 1–0 win in the opener but lost its other two matches, 1–0 to Poland and 3–1 to Morocco.

2. **ITALIAN FANS**

Italy was expected to field a strong, star-filled World Cup team in England in 1966 but won only one match and lost two, including a shocking 1–0 loss to North Korea. Frightened by the negative reaction of their countrymen, the Italian team jettisoned a plan to return to Rome in midday and instead routed the team plane to Genoa in the middle of the night. The ruse didn't work, however, as the players were greeted with a barrage of rotten vegetables, many of which were better aimed than the team's shots on goal during the tournament. For months, members of the Italian World Cup team were booed whenever they appeared in a league match.

3. **PRINCE FAHID OF KUWAIT**

France was leading Kuwait 3–1 in the 80th minute in the 1982 World Cup in Spain when France's Alain Giresse accepted a pass from Michael Platini and volleyed in an apparent goal. The Kuwaiti players argued with referee Miroslav Stupor of the Soviet Union that a spectator with a whistle caused them to stop, believing Giresse was offside. During the protest, Prince Fahid of Kuwait, who was also the president of his country's FA and one of the world's richest men, went onto the field to appeal to the referee. The goal was disallowed much to the consternation of the French, but they scored again to win 4–1.

4. **JIMMY KEMP**

Jimmy Kemp, a Scottish hospital cook, was so distraught by Scotland's play in the 1978 World Cup that he purchased space in a local newspaper to announce that in the future he wished to be regarded as an Englishman. Kemp also said that he would be taking elocution lessons to rid himself of his Scottish accent.

5. **ANTHONY DE AVILA**

Colombia's Anthony de Avila took the occasion of a victory and a goal he scored against Ecuador in World Cup qualifying on June 20, 1997, to protest the incarceration of Miguel and Gilberto Rodriguez Orejuela, a pair of brothers who headed the Cali drug cartel before they were arrested in 1995. "I'd like to dedicate the goal," said de Avila, "to all those who for some reason or another are denied their freedom."

6. FLUMINENSE

Supporters of the normally dominant Fluminense club in soccer-mad Brazil were so fed up with their team's play that only 22 fans showed up for a 1–0 victory over Volta Redonda on April 17, 1996.

7. GREEK FARMERS

Thousands of protesting farmers blocked all the exits from the town of Larissa, Greece, on March 26, 1995, and prevented the local soccer club from traveling to play a Greek First Division match against OFI on the island of Crete. The match had to postponed because Larissa missed the plane. The farmers had blocked the main highway linking Athens and the northern part of Salonika in protest of a new law requiring higher taxes.

8. PETER LEWIS

Peter Lewis, the public-address announcer for Swindon Town in England, was fired at halftime of a match against Bolton on April 5, 1995, for criticizing referee Graham Baker. "I've seen some crap refereeing decisions in my time, but...," Lewis shouted into the stadium microphone before he was drowned out by cheers from the approving crowd. Bolton won the match 1–0.

9. **HONDURAN FANS**

On February 20, 2000, scores of Honduran fans showed
their distaste with refereeing decisions that led to a 5–3
defeat against Peru in the Gold Cup at the Orange Bowl in
Miami by ripping up seats, fighting with police, and throwing
rocks and bottles.

10. **HONDURAS**

During World Cup qualifying in 1996, Rudolfo Richardson
Smith of Honduras, a national-team veteran and one of the
top midfielders in Central America, lost control of the ball to
a Mexican player on the edge of the penalty area, a mistake
which led to a goal. Honduras went on to lose 3–1. After the
match, fans threw bottles and firecrackers at Richardson
Smith's residence in San Pedro Sula and continued to taunt
him and his family for weeks. He finally moved to El Salvador.

Air Disasters

Plane crashes have been an unfortunate by-product of matches being played all over the world.

1. TORINO

Many of the best players in Italy were killed on May 4, 1949, when a plane carrying the Torino club home from a charity match in Portugal crashed into the side of the basilica on top of Superga Hill outside Turin. When the plane crashed, it was heading in the wrong direction, a mystery that has never been explained. Eighteen players were killed, including the bulk of Italy's national team. Torino had won four consecutive Italian League titles and was in first place on the day of the crash. The Torino youth team finished the season and received the championship trophy.

2. MANCHESTER UNITED

In 1958 Manchester United's plane crashed on takeoff at the snowy Munich, West Germany, airport killing eight members of the team. Manchester United was returning to England from a 3–3 draw with Red Star Belgrade in Yugoslavia which earned them a place in the European Cup finals. With a group of players known as "Busby's Babes," after coach Matt Busby, Manchester United had won the championship of England in 1952, 1956, and 1957.

3. ZAMBIA

The Zambian national team died in a crash just before midnight on April 27, 1993, as the plane dropped into the Atlantic Ocean off the coast of Gabon. All 18 players, the coaches, and the trainer were buried together outside Independence Stadium in Lusaka. A new team was formed to qualify for the World Cup and fought gamely, including a 4–0 win over Senegal, but was eliminated in a 1–0 loss to Morocco. Zambia reached the African Nations' Cup in 1994 but lost 2–1 to Nigeria in Tunisia.

4. CHILE

An airplane crash into the Las Lastimas Mountain killed 24 members of the Green Cross club in Chile in 1962 on their way from Santiago to Orsono for the Chile Cup playoffs.

5. BOLIVIA

Nineteen players and officials from The Strongest, Bolivia's most popular club, died in 1969 when their plane crashed in the Andes Mountains 72 miles from their destination at La Paz.

6. SOVIET UNION

Seventeen players of Pakhtakor Tashkent of the Soviet Union were killed on their way to a league match in 1979 along with 237 others in a midair collision between two planes. The Soviet government kept the disaster a state secret for several years.

7. **PERU**

Players, officials, and supporters of the Alianza team in Lima, Peru, died in 1987 while returning from a league game. The plane crashed into the sea in foggy weather six miles north of the Peruvian capital. The death toll included 17 players, six officials, four trainers, three referees, eight fans, and five crew members.

8. **ALGERIA**

The amateur club Air Liquide of Algeria perished on December 31, 1970, when its plane crashed into the Mediterranean Sea en route to Spain to play a friendly, which had been arranged by club officials as a gesture of gratitude to players for their loyalty and service to the club.

9. **DENMARK**

Eight of Denmark's leading soccer players, including six members of the national team, were killed in a chartered plane in 1960 that crashed after taking off from a runway at Copenhagen Airport.

10. **SURINAME**

In 1989, 14 players from Suriname died in a jetliner en route from the Netherlands at Paramaribo International Airport.

Against All Odds

Many teams and players have overcome long odds, hardships, or seemingly insurmountable obstacles to achieve success.

1. GARRINCHA

Born Manoel dos Santos Francisco in Brazil, Garrincha became a soccer star despite a childhood bout with polio, which made one of his legs shorter than the other. Garrincha is a Portuguese expression for "useless little bird." As a result of his illness, Garrincha's movements on the field were unpredictable and very difficult to defend. He played for two of Brazil's World Cup champions in 1958 and 1962 and scored two goals in the 1962 final. Garrincha also played on Brazil's losing effort in 1966, coming back from knee surgery and overcoming a scandal in which he left his wife and eight children to marry a singer. He died virtually penniless at the age of 49 in 1983.

2. SALVATORE SCHILLACI

Salvatore Schillaci was the last player chosen for the 1990 Italian World Cup team. He began the tournament on the bench and finished as the leading scorer of the tournament with six goals. Schillaci entered the first game against Austria as a 74th-minute substitute, and four minutes later he scored the only goal of the match to give Italy a 1–0 win. Schillaci didn't earn a start until Italy's third game, but he scored a goal in each of his country's final five matches, including the third-place playoff in which Italy defeated England 2–1.

3. DENMARK, 1992

Denmark failed to qualify for the final stages of the 1992 European championships but got in when war-ravaged Yugoslavia had to withdraw. Many Danish players had been on vacation and were out of condition when the call came to travel to Sweden to compete for the continental championship. The team didn't assemble for practice until nine days before the start of the tournament. Denmark began auspiciously with a tie against England and a loss to Sweden before defeating France on a late goal. The victory over France put Denmark in second place in its group and earned the team a spot in the semifinals. The Danes defeated the Netherlands on penalty kicks in the semis and met Germany in the final as a huge underdog. Nonetheless, Denmark completed its bizarre journey by stunning the Germans 2–0 to win the championship.

4. SUNDERLAND, 1973

Six months after being one of the low-end clubs in England's Second Division, Sunderland won the FA Cup in 1973 as a 250–1 underdog. In the final, Sunderland beat Leeds United, then one of the top teams in Europe, 1–0. On the way to the winning the trophy, Sunderland also knocked off Arsenal and Manchester City. The previous November and December,

Sunderland lost 10 matches in a row, but after Bob Stokoe took over as manager, won 10 in succession.

5. **WALES, 1958**

Wales qualified for the final round of the World Cup in 1958 for the only time in history, doing so in a roundabout way. Wales finished second in its qualifying group and was therefore eliminated. But the Welsh team was chosen in a lottery among the 13 second-place teams around the world to face Israel in a three-match playoff. Wales won the series to earn a berth in Sweden. Once there, Wales reached the quarterfinals with a win and three draws before being knocked out of the tournament by Brazil 1–0 on a goal by Pele.

6. **ITALY, 1994**

In a second-round match against Nigeria in the 1994 World Cup in Foxboro, Massachusetts, Italy was on the verge of elimination facing a 1–0 deficit when Roberto Baggio scored in the 89th minute. In extra time, Baggio converted a penalty kick to give the Italians a 2–1 victory. Spurred on by the comeback win, Italy reached the final against Brazil but lost in the penalty-kick round. Ironically, the match ended when Baggio missed a shot.

7. **ARSENAL, 1989**

Arsenal needed to win its final match of the 1988–89 season against Liverpool by two goals to capture England's Premier League championship. The match was played at Liverpool's Anfield Road, where the home club had a 10-game winning streak. Arsenal went up 1–0 in the 58th minute on an Alan Smith score. Two minutes into stoppage time Michael Thomas put the ball into the net on a breakaway to give Arsenal a

2−0 lead. Seconds later, the referee signalled the end of the match, and Arsenal had the title.

8. **HARTWICK COLLEGE**

Tiny Hartwick College, located in Oneonta, New York, with an enrollment of 1,450, won the 1977 NCAA championship with a record of 16-0-2.

9. **UNIVERSITY OF FLORIDA, 1998**

The women's soccer program at the University of Florida was only in its fourth year when it won the NCAA championship with a 1−0 win over North Carolina. The Tar Heels had won 14 of the previous 16 collegiate titles. Becky Burleigh, Florida's coach, also became the first woman to coach an NCAA soccer champion.

10. **WEST HAM UNITED, 1980**

West Ham United won the English FA Cup in 1980 as a Second Division club, defeating odds-on favorite Arsenal 1−0. The only goal was scored in the 14th minute by 35-year-old Trevor Brooking, the oldest player on the field.

Food for Thought

The dietary patterns of players and fans all over the world have long been the subject of discussion.

1. EGYPT AND ZAIRE

Zaire reached the final round of the World Cup for the only time in its history in 1974. In March of that year, Zaire played a preparatory match against Egypt's national team in Alexandria. Cooks at the Zaire team's hotel protested when they were asked to prepare the visitor's national dish—monkeys brought from Zaire skinned and dressed. Hotel management agreed to allow the players to prepare their own meals in the hotel kitchen, provided they dined in their rooms.

2. SOUTH KOREA

South Korean lawmakers, acting on a bill before the National Assembly on September 27, 1999, refused to legalize the sale of dog meat, considered a delicacy by many Koreans, before the 2002 World Cup finals got underway. The Ministry of Agriculture and Forestry said that authorizing the sale of dog flesh would give South Korea a bad international image. South Korea also forbade the consumption of dog meat during the 1988 Olympics in Seoul, but the old practice was tolerated afterwards.

3. FABRIZIO RAVANELLI

The contract of Fabrizio Ravanelli was sold by Juventus to England's Middlesbrough club in 1996, and he wasn't happy about it. Still, Ravanelli tried to make the best of the situation and scored three goals in his home debut against Liverpool. He grew increasingly disenchanted with England over the course of the season, though, and was especially disgusted by the training habits of the English players, which included consuming large quantities of bacon, fish and chips, and beer.

4. ALDERSHOT

It's a good thing that Fabrizio Ravanelli didn't play for England's Aldershot club in 1933. During the FA Cup tournament that year, Aldershot decided to experiment by ending practice sessions with sherry-and-egg cocktails.

5. ROBERTO ACUNA

Roberto Acuna walked out on the Paraguayan national team on the eve of the 1999 Copa America because coach Ever Almeida insisted that his players eat nothing but fish.

6. JIM STANNARD

English Second Division club Gillingham warned fans in 1996 that they would be banned for life if they brought celery into the stands. As they entered the gates, fans were frisked for the vegetable because the club's hefty goalkeeper, Jim Stannard, had been pelted with celery as a suggestion that he lose weight. "Fat chance of me going on a diet," said Stannard. "I like my pasta too much. Perhaps if they threw lasagna, I might take notice."

7. ENGLAND

Skeptical of Mexican cuisine, England's players brought their own bacon, sausage, and bottled water to the World Cup in 1970, but the food supplies were destroyed in customs as prescribed by Mexican law.

8. DEAD FISH

During a 2000 friendly in Budapest between Australia and Hungary, fans threw dead fish at the Australian players. The action was in protest of a cyanide spill from a tailing dam owned by an Australian company that killed thousands of fish and devastated other wildlife in Hungary's Tisza River. Australia avoided the hail of dead fish long enough to win the match 3–0.

9. CARLOS BILARDO

Argentina's national team coach, Carlos Bilardo, wouldn't let his players eat chicken during the 1986 and 1990 World Cups because he considered it to be bad luck. It certainly worked in 1986, when Argentina won the tournament. In 1990, the team reached the final, where they lost to West Germany 1–0.

10. ROBERT PROSNECKI

Robert Prosnecki is the only player to score goals in a World Cup final round for two different countries, doing so for Yugoslavia in 1990 and Croatia in 1998. He became wealthy playing for top clubs in Spain and was so anxious to return home that he signed an unusual contract for the Croatian First Division club Hrvatski Dragovoljac in 2000. If the team won the match, Prosnecki received a free lunch. If they lost, Prosnecki bought lunch for the entire team.

Good Old-Time Religion

With so many cultures playing soccer around the world, religious conflicts are bound to occur.

1. HEART OF MIDLOTHIAN

In Edinburgh, Scotland, many of the worshippers at a church next to the Heart of Midlothian club's stadium, Tynecastle Park, were too frightened to attend Sunday evening services when the team was playing at home. In 2000, the church minister asked the Hearts not to play on Sunday nights because the elderly parishioners feared the crowds. Services were frequently interrupted by wild cheering emanating from the stadium. The Hearts said that the Sunday evening scheduling slot was dictated by television.

2. DAVID BECKHAM

England's star player David Beckham was immortalized in 2000 by a fan in Thailand inside a Buddhist temple at a spot normally reserved for religious figures. The one-foot-high statue was covered in gold leaf and placed at the foot of the main Buddha image in Bangkok's Pariwas Temple. "Football," explained the temple's senior monk, "has become a religion and has millions of followers."

3. GLENN HODDLE

England's national coach, Glenn Hoddle, was fired in February 1999, for commenting that disabled people were paying for "sins of an earlier life" and that their disabilities were the result of "bad karma." Hoddle was a born-again Christian who believed in reincarnation and spiritual healing.

4. PAUL GASCOIGNE

Playing for the Rangers in Glasgow, Paul Gascoigne had to apologize to Catholics in 1998 for miming a flute player during the traditional New Years' Day match between the Rangers and the Celtic. The flute is a symbol of Protestant marches favored by Rangers fans and considered inflammatory to the mainly Catholic fans of Celtic. Gascoigne was fined $32,200 by the Rangers. Earlier, he had performed the same routine during a match in England in 1995.

5. GERMANS IN ISRAEL

The German national team played an exhibition match in Israel in 1997 and took time out to tour the Yad Vashern Holocaust Memorial in Jerusalem where players laid a wreath in memory of the six million Jews killed in the Nazi genocide. "It was very, very emotional and almost shocking," said German team player Jurgen Klinsmann, who also took time to sign autographs at the site. "Even if we are a younger generation, we still have the responsibility to teach the next generation everything that happened to them 50 years ago."

6. DUNCAN EDWARDS

Duncan Edwards was already one of England's best players at the age of 21 when he was killed in the Manchester United plane crash in 1958. A picture of him in his Manchester United uniform was made part of a stained-glass window erected in his memory at his local church at Dudley in Worcestershire.

7. NUN-SENSE

On June 21, 1978, a nun in a Frankfurt, West Germany, cafe was arrested when she attempted to strangle a man when he cheered for Austria's 3–2 World Cup victory over West Germany.

8. PRIESTS VS. COMMUNISTS

In 1958 in Italy, a match was contested between black-robed priests and the communist and socialist mayors and council-men of the towns and villages near Bardineto. The priests and the communists had been involved in a number of political spats, and it was decided they would settle their differences on the soccer field. The match ended in a 3–3 tie before a crowd of 3,000. The priests' attack was led by 50-year-old Don Sofia, rector of the parish of Calizzano.

9. VIENNA, AUSTRIA

A match in Vienna, Austria, on March 26, 1946, between the Jewish Sports Club Hakoah and the Police Sports Club result-ed in a riot between Jewish and Gentile fans. The police riot squad had to be called to quell the disturbance. One Jewish spectator asked a security guard to take the name of a man who shouted an anti-Semitic insult at the Jewish team. Part of the crowd began to shout "into the gas with them" in reference to the Nazi gas chambers of World War II, which had ended less than a year earlier.

10. **RONALDO**

Brazilian star Ronaldo appeared as Christ in a promotional poster for his club, Inter Milan, in Italy in 1998. Many considered the poster to be blasphemous. The poster depicted Ronaldo with his arms outstretched gazing down on Rio de Janeiro in an imitation of the huge statue of Christ the Redeemer that overlooks the Brazilian city from the summit of Corcovado Mountain.

Soccer in Iran

The combination of a fundamentalist Islamic theocracy and the tremendous popularity of soccer in Iran has led to some unique moments.

1. AYATOLLAH KHOMENI

When the Ayatollah Khomeni took over the Iranian government in 1979, one of his first pronouncements was to prohibit soccer as an insidious western influence. The game was too popular to be stamped out, however, and the country's religious rulers had to accede to the will of the people. Soccer has flourished in Iran and is played in the streets in virtually every city, town, and village.

2. TELEVISION

During the 1994 World Cup, Iranian television broadcast the games on a slight delay to avoid showing women in the stands wearing shorts and T-shirts in violation of the strict Islamic dress code. When shots of the crowds in the U.S. stadiums were shown, they were replaced by replays of previous action.

3. **HABIB KHABARI**

Iranian soccer hero Habib Khabari scored a dramatic goal from 40 yards out in 1977 in qualifying against Kuwait to put Iran into the World Cup final round for the first time. In 1979, after the Shah abdicated and the fundamentalists took over, Khabari was arrested as an enemy of the new regime. In 1984, he was told he would be set free the next day. When awakened, Khabari was taken to a wall and executed.

4. **IRANIAN WOMEN**

Iran prevented women from attending celebrations at Azadi Stadium in Teheran on December 2, 1997, after Iran qualified for the World Cup final round. Iranian soccer federation officials released a statement read on state television and radio stations: "In view of the lack of suitable space and in order to safeguard Islamic dignity, sisters will be strictly prevented from entering Azadi Stadium. Sisters can witness the fervent celebrations on live television at home." About 3,000 women poured into the stadium in defiance of the ban, however, many of them disguised as men. Once inside, they were herded into a special section segregated from male fans.

5. **EXAMS**

In 1994, Iran's Education Ministry ordered some high-school graduation exams for boys be moved up so they wouldn't coincide with World Cup matches. The change was made even though the Iranian team wasn't participating, and the tournament was being played in the dreaded United States. Education Minister Mohammed Ali Najafi said the ministry feared a "drop in performance" if the exams were held after the June 12 opening of the World Cup.

6. GOLAGHA

The Iranian magazine *Golagha* in 1992 printed a cartoon of the Ayatollah Khomeni dressed in a soccer uniform. The magazine's office was promptly destroyed by religious fanatics and its editors jailed.

7. IRAQ VS. IRAN

Iran and Iraq met in World Cup qualifying on October 22, 1993, in Doha, Qatar, in the first official match since the two countries fought a bitter war which lasted from 1980 until 1988. Security was tight because fans from both countries were in the stands, but the match was surprisingly peaceful. Iraq won 2–1, but neither team advanced to the final round.

8. UNITED STATES VS. IRAN

The meeting between the United States and Iran during the 1998 World Cup in France brought new meaning to the term "political football." On June 21, Iran stunned the Americans 2–1. It was Iran's first-ever win in the final rounds of the World Cup tournament and knocked the U.S. out of contention for a spot in the second round. There were fears that the match would deepen the rift between the two countries, but the fears proved unfounded. Prior to the contest, Iranian players shook hands with the American players and handed them white flowers.

9. MEHDI MAHDAVIKIA

Iranian soccer player Mehdi Mahdavikia was exempted from military service in gratitude for scoring the winning goal against the United States during the 1998 World Cup.

10. **DRESS**

Many of Iran's religious leaders believe that traditional soccer garb exposes too much flesh. They have tried to persuade players and soccer officials to dress the athletes in long-sleeved warm-up outfits for matches but have been unsuccessful. The Islamic dress code has been an extreme hindrance to Iran starting a soccer program for women.

Curses, Spells, and Lucky Charms

M any believe their success or failure on the soccer field
has been the result of a curse or lucky charm.

1. PEREIRA

The Colombian First Division club Pereira won only two of its
first 14 matches in 1997 and believed it was a victim of witch-
craft after a dead black chicken was found in a luxury box
at the club's Hernen Ramirez Stadium. Club president Augusto
Ramirez said the animal had been strung up with lighting
cable and that three black bags containing earth from a
nearby cemetery were also found lined up with "some mark-
ings which we could not understand." Ramirez said he would
organize a ceremony to ward off evil spirits.

2. THE CANALES BROTHERS

Augusto and Ramon Canales were retained by the Peruvians
during the World Cup in 1982 to put a hex on opponents by
means of special herbs, clay dolls, and magic rattles. They
were unsuccessful. Peru tied Cameroon 0–0 and Italy 1–1
and lost 5–1 to Poland, a game in which the Poles scored all
of their goals during a 22-minute stretch of the second half.

3. **VASCO DA GAMA**

In 1937, a rival fan of the Vasco da Gama club in Rio de Janeiro, Brazil, buried a toad with its mouth sewed shut beneath Vasco da Gama's playing field, called down a curse, and claimed that the team wouldn't win a championship for 12 years. For years, fans and players of Vasco da Gama dug up the playing field looking for the toad. It was never found, though several players were injured as a result of running across a field pockmarked with divots. Apparently, the curse was good only for eight years, because Vasco da Gama won the Rio trophy in 1945.

4. **FREDDY RINCON**

Colombia's Freddy Rincon consulted a prophet from his hometown of Buenaventura before the 1994 World Cup. The prophet foretold the results of the tournament exactly as they happened, including Colombia's unexpected bounce from the competition in the first round. The soothsayer also said that Rincon would break his leg if he wasn't careful, and the player studiously avoided contact whenever possible.

5. **ATUAULFO VALENCIA**

Ecuador's Atuaulfo Valencia claimed he was cursed after an incident in 1996. He was run over by a cart that had been driven onto the field to carry off an injured player near the end of the Copa Libertadores match between his Espoli club and Ecuadorian rival Barcelona. To compound his problems, Valencia was red carded by the referee when he lashed out at the driver.

6. **AFRICA**

Many African clubs make room in their budgets for magic and solicit advice from witch doctors before matches.

Kenyan players have been known to coat their bodies with pig fat, a remedy believed to repel spells and charms. Sentries have been posted to patrol stadiums and make certain that no one places a charm upon the ball. Many clubs avoid the locker rooms in opposing stadiums for fear of evil charms left there by rivals.

7. SOUTH AFRICA

The start of a match in South Africa in 1995 was delayed 10 minutes after the visiting team accused its host of using magical powers against it. The match pitted the host Moroka Swallows against the heavily favored Qwa Qwa Stars in Soweto. The Stars players claimed a Swallows official had splashed "magical water" on them before the start of the match and had threatened them with a knobkerrie, a traditional African fighting stick. A Swallows official had also sprinkled the water in the Stars' goal mouth. The match was delayed to allow the shirts of the Qwa Qwa players to dry. The contest ended in a 1–1 draw.

8. DERBY COUNTY

From 1895 until 1997, England's Derby County club played at a stadium known as the Baseball Grounds. Club president Francis Ley had fallen in love with baseball during a trip to the United States and resolved to convert Britishers to the game. Ley gave up his losing battle to bring baseball to England during the 1920s, but up until that time, both soccer and baseball were played at the Baseball Grounds. The stadium name remained for more than 70 years. The terraces at the home-plate end of the stands were known as Catcher's Corner. When Ley first laid out his grounds, he allegedly drove out a Gypsy community which then placed a curse on the club. In 1946, with members of the press looking on, club captain Jack Nicholas crossed a Gypsy's palm with silver in order to lift the curse. Derby County went on to win the FA Cup for the only time in its history.

9. ROMANIA

The Romanian national team trained in Budapest, Hungary, in 1998 for friendlies against Greece and Israel in preparation for the World Cup but moved to another location because the training camp was too close to a cemetery. The Romanians blamed a 1–0 loss to Israel on the "lugubrious atmosphere" of the camp, especially at sunset.

10. NIGERIA

In 1983, the players of the Stationery Stores club of Nigeria attacked the opposing goalkeeper because they believed he had planted a magic charm in his goal. The Confederation of African Football suspended the players for two years.

Suspensions and Banishments

Many players and teams have reacted badly to adverse conditions, necessitating punishment by the proper authorities.

1. STAN COLLYMORE

In February 2000, seven days after joining England's Leicester City club from Aston Villa, Stan Collymore was suspended for two weeks for setting off a fire extinguisher at the club's training camp in La Marga, Spain. "To be honest," said team coach Martin O'Neill, "I always felt that when we signed him that sooner or later he would be involved in some sort of incident that would hit the headlines. I just did not expect it to happen so quickly."

2. ERIC CANTONA

At his peak, French-born Eric Cantona was one of the world's best players, but he also possessed a world-class temper. In January 1995, while playing for Manchester United, Cantona flew into the stands feetfirst to assault a heckling fan during a match against Crystal Palace. The *kung fu* kick earned

Cantona a nine-month worldwide ban from FIFA. He also received a two-week jail sentence for assault, later commuted to 120 hours of community service.

3. DIEGO MARADONA

Argentina's Diego Maradona was another world-class player who ran afoul of FIFA. Soccer's governing body suspended him for 15 months in 1994 for cocaine use. Maradona holds the unofficial world record for bad career moves. In 1998, he hired sprinter Ben Johnson to serve as his personal trainer after Johnson had been banned for life by the International Amateur Athletic Association for using performance-enhancing drugs. Still struggling in 2000, Maradona went to Cuba because of his friendship with Fidel Castro to undergo drug rehabilitation.

4. WENCESLAO AGUILERA PEDEROS

Trainer for Chile's Iberia team, Wenceslao Aguilera Pederos was suspended for life after giving his team sleeping pills before a match in 1993. He was bribed $250 by fans of an opposing team prior to a match that would determine which club would earn a promotion to Chile's Second Division. Pederos told the Iberia players the pills were Vitamin C tablets. Iberia snoozed to a 3–0 loss.

5. VINNIE JONES

Wimbledon star Vinnie Jones was suspended for six months by the English FA in 1992 for "bringing the game into disrepute." Jones narrated a video titled *Soccer's Hard Men,* which featured players elbowing opponents, pulling armpit hair, raking their boot studs down calves, and grabbing genitals (which he did to Paul Gascoigne). Jones was fined heavily a year earlier for making obscene gestures in the direction of Chelsea fans. Nowadays, Vinnie has taken his rough act to the silver screen, where he has made memorable appearances in *Lock, Stock and Two Smoking Barrels* and *Snatch.* The director of both films was Guy Ritchie. In January 2001, Ritchie married Madonna and wanted Jones as his best man, but the former soccer star couldn't attend the nuptials because he was making another movie in Los Angeles.

6. ANDRES MAZZALI

Andres Mazzali starred for the Uruguayan team in goal in both the 1924 and 1928 Olympics. He led his nation to two gold medals, allowing just seven goals in 10 matches. He was expected to do the same at the World Cup in 1930 but was kicked off the team during training after sneaking out of the team hotel to visit his family. Mazzali was homesick because the Uruguayans had been training for two months for the tournament in a luxury hotel in Prado Park in Montevideo.

7. ERNST JEAN-JOSEPH

Ernst Jean-Joseph of Haiti was the first player to be suspended by the FIFA for drug use during the World Cup. The suspension occurred on June 18, 1974, after a routine drug test. Jean-Joseph had ingested a stimulant containing phenylmetrazin.

8. LIAM DAISH

Liam Daish, captain of English Second Division club Birmingham City, was suspended for two matches in 1994 for playing a trumpet. Daish played the instrument, which was handed to him by a fan, in celebration of a goal scored by a teammate in a 4–0 win over Chester.

9. LUIGI COLUCCIO

Italian amateur player Luigi Coluccio was given a one-match ban nine days after he was shot dead outside a bar in Southern Italy. Coluccio was killed on November 1, 1995, while closing up a bar he owned in the town of Gioiosa Jonica. Police thought the shooting appeared to be connected with an extortion racket linked to a local mob. Three days before his death, Coluccio had been sent off the field during an amateur match while playing for his hometown against Bocal. On November 10, the league president decided that procedures must be followed, and despite Coluccio's demise and his obvious inability to perform, the president issued the order to suspend the player.

10. KURT ROETHLISBERGER

Swiss referee Kurt Roethlisberger was banned for life by the UEFA in March 1997 for attempted bribery involving a championship match between Grasshopper Zurich and Auxerre played on October 30, 1996. Roethlisberger contacted Grasshopper coach Erich Vogel and visited his office on October 18. Roethlisberger told Vogel that the referee assigned to the match wouldn't make decisions against the Grasshopper club in exchange for $68,600. Grasshopper won 3–1.

Hoaxes, Myths, and Mistaken Identity

S ometimes, things are not what they seem to be.

1. **BOBBY MOORE**

England's Bobby Moore was voted the outstanding player of the 1966 World Cup and was a member of the English team again four years later. On a tour of Colombia prior to the 1970 tournament in Mexico, Moore was accused of stealing a bracelet from a jewelry store in Bogata, where the English team was staying. Moore was detained for four days before being released in time to play in the World Cup. Moore was acquitted of all charges when it was revealed he had been framed.

2. **ROBERTO ROJAS**

Brazil led Chile 1–0 with 22 minutes remaining during a World Cup qualifying match in Rio De Janeiro on September 3, 1989, when a flare landed near Chilean goalkeeper Roberto Rojas. He promptly fell backward and held his face in his hands. The Chileans left the field and didn't return, citing concern for their safety. Doctors examined Rojas and said he had a cut on his forehead but no burns. The FIFA awarded the match to Brazil and eliminated Chile from the tournament. Rojas was banned for life for faking the injury.

3. ROSEMARY DE MELLO

It was Rosemary de Mello who threw the flare that caused the controversy at the 1989 Brazil-Chile match. Afterward, she appeared in television commercials and received an offer from the editor of the Brazilian edition of *Playboy* to pose for a centerfold. Known as "Rocket Rosey," she did one TV ad for a travel agency announcing that she was going to the World Cup the following summer in Italy, but without her fireworks.

4. OTTORINO BARASSI

After winning the World Cup in 1938, Italy ended up with the trophy for 12 years because of World War II, which prevented the tournament from being staged in 1942 and 1946. A myth grew that Ottorino Barassi, head of Italian Sport, feared the Nazis would confiscate the trophy, so for the remainder of World War II, he kept the valued piece of hardware in a shoebox under his bed. Others report that it was actually Jules Rimet, FIFA president, who kept the trophy hidden under his bed in France. It was actually stored in a Rome bank vault.

5. DYNAMO KIEV

According to legend, the Germans played a soccer match against the powerful Dynamo Kiev team during the Nazi occupation of the Ukraine in 1942. After the Dynamo team won, they were marched to the edge of a cliff and shot to death while still in full uniform. The Soviets made a huge propaganda issue out of the alleged incident, but there's no solid historical evidence that the match ever took place.

6. SOVIET UNION

Two Moscow residents made a fortune in 1959 by touring remote cities of the Soviet Union with a mediocre team posing as the famous Dynamo squad. The team was beaten by most local clubs; the promoters explained that the team was merely off form. The fate of the promoters is unknown, but they no doubt spent many years touring remote Siberian prison camps.

7. SOL FOX

During World War II, American First Lieutenant Sol Fox was shot down with his crew in a B-17 over Romania in July 1944. Fox was taken prisoner, and the major in charge of the camp mistook him for a soccer star he'd seen play in Vienna in 1938. Fox protested that he was an American and had never played soccer, but the major refused to believe him and said he would honor Fox's wish to keep his "identity" a secret. Fox and his crew were in camp for four days and were treated to sumptuous feasts before being transferred to Bucharest and put on short rations.

8. EL SALVADOR

A squad from the far-right-wing National Republic Alliance faced a team of purported communists in San Salvador, El Salvador, before a crowd of 30,000 at Flor Blanca Stadium on March 11, 1984. The match was part of the campaign of NRA presidential candidate Roberto d'Aubuisson. The "communist" players were actually supporters of d'Aubuisson and had about as much chance of winning as the Washington

Generals had of defeating the Harlem Globetrotters. Candidate d'Aubuisson hoped the 8–2 victory over the "communists" would demonstrate the righteousness of his cause, but he lost the election to Jose Napoleon Duarte.

9. BURMA

During the long postwar civil disturbances in Burma, a Karen battalion in lower Burma invited a group of communist insurgents for a "friendly" game on March 22, 1955. Just before the scheduled kickoff, the Karens led their opponents into the jungle and bound them hand and foot before shooting them. The Karens also made off with the money the communists had waged on the match.

10. CANADA

Thousands of Canadians were thrilled in March 1982 by newspaper accounts of an Ontario teenager who reportedly led the country's junior soccer team to a world championship in a tournament in Sydney, Australia. The tournament turned out to be part of an elaborate hoax staged by the teenager in an attempt to win the sportsman-of-the-year award in his hometown. Victor Notaro, a 19-year-old from Weiland, Ontario, played at Western Michigan University and phoned reports back to his hometown newspaper about his exploits in the fictitious competition. The articles were written by the sports editor of the *Weiland Tribune,* who passed the information along to other newspapers. The *Toronto Star,* Canada's largest newspaper, also printed the story without bothering to check the facts.

Promotional Exercises

Soccer has spawned some bizarre promotional schemes.

1. FULHAM

A Second Division club in England, Fulham required fans to pass a trivia quiz before they could purchase tickets for an English FA Cup match against Manchester United in 1999. The London-based club quizzed prospective ticket buyers to ensure that tickets for Fulham's biggest match in years would go to genuine fans. The club is owned by Mohammed Al Fayed, whose son Dodi was killed in the Paris car crash that also claimed the life of Princess Diana in 1996.

2. COVENTRY CITY

In 1999, Coventry City in England's Premier League launched an official club condom. "This is not a joke product," said the head of the Coventry City's retail operations. "We are a responsible club." The condoms were sold in vending machines at the club's Highfield Road Stadium.

3. **AUSTRALIA**

Twelve members of Australia's women's team, looking to generate publicity, posed nude for a 2000 calendar. "It's all about boosting the profile of the team and our sport, and it looks like we're going to achieve that," said midfielder Alison Forman. The calendar was unveiled at a December 1, 1999, press conference.

4. **POCKET KNIVES**

As if soccer didn't have enough problems with fan violence, the French FA sanctioned the sale of souvenir World Cup pocket knives in 1998. The FIFA stopped the sale of the weapons, but not before they appeared in stores throughout France. The knives contained a four-inch blade of a type that is illegal in Britain.

5. **FRENCH TOURISM**

Many observers predicted a 30 percent drop in tourism in France in 1998, citing tourist fears of violence during the World Cup. The province of Alsace on the eastern border with Germany was one of the few areas of France not hosting a World Cup match. Oliver de Richoulitz, Alsatian tourism director, billed the locale as a "soccer-free zone." Flyers were sent out hyping the region's clear lakes, blue skies, and medieval fairs.

6. **TONY MEOLA**

To generate publicity for the United States–Germany match at Soldier Field in Chicago in 1993, U.S. soccer officials arranged for goalkeeper Tony Meola to kick balls 70 yards across the Chicago River. The first three attempts ended up in the water two-thirds of the way across. Meola finally made it on the fourth try on a kick that just cleared the railing on the opposite bank.

7. ITALIAN STRIPTEASE ARTISTS

In 1996, male striptease artists in Italy formed a national team to play matches for charity. The team competed in conventional soccer uniforms instead of their usual working attire. "No loin cloths. We preferred a classical uniform," said the team captain. "After all, we are professional strip-artists, not gigolos." The club was coached by former pro player Enzo Romano. "It's an opportunity to get together and help those in need and maybe regain some image," said one player.

8. UNITED ARAB EMIRATES

A car dealership in the United Arab Emirates bought all of the tickets to the semifinals and finals of the 1996 Asian Cup. The Al-Masood car dealers paid $280,000 for the tickets, which were given away to customers in the dealership's showrooms.

9. ROME

After the 1990 World Cup, chunks of turf from the Olympic Stadium in Rome, where the final was held, were sold. The sale netted $5.8 million.

10. GERMANY

Tolerance was the theme on the final game day of Germany's Bundesliga in 1992. Players on all 18 clubs in the league bore the slogan "Together in Peace" on the fronts of their jerseys. The promotion was in response to a rise of neo-Nazism in Germany. Foreign players had been subjected to racist chants and signs at the nation's soccer stadiums, especially those players from Africa.

Security!

Deaths inside soccer stadiums have been an all too frequent occurrence.

1. COLOMBIA

On November 18, 1982, 22 spectators were killed as a result of a stampede in Cali, Colombia. The disaster was triggered by a group of intoxicated youths in the upper level of Pascual Uerrero Stadium who threw trash and urinated over thousands of people heading for the exits after a pro match between Deportivo Cali and America ended in a 3–3 draw. Seven children were among those who died.

2. GUATEMALA

On October 16, 1996, at Mateo Flores Stadium in Guatemala City, Guatemala, 84 fans perished in a melee prior to a World Cup qualifying match against Costa Rica. Because forgers sold fake tickets to the event, an estimated 60,000 had squeezed into a venue designed to hold 45,000. The disaster occurred when fans escaping a drunken brawl crushed and smothered one another against a chain-link fence at the base of the stands.

3. **HONDURAS**

Lightning killed 17 people at a soccer match on June 3, 1996, in the Honduran town of Puerto Lempira. Fans were huddled under a shelter beside the soccer field when the bolt struck. Lack of adequate medical facilities added to the tragedy. Puerto Lempira is a remote Atlantic coast fishing town with few basic services and access only by boat.

4. **LIBYA**

In 1996, at least 20 people were killed at a soccer match in Tripoli, Libya, after bodyguards loyal to the sons of Libyan leader Colonel Muammar el-Qaddafi fired at spectators who were shouting hostile slogans. The fans began shouting after the referee made several dubious decisions in favor of the team that the Libyan leader's sons were supporting. Some fans returned the gunfire, causing widespread panic. During the violence, fans ran onto the field and stabbed the referee. The rioters then spilled into the streets and began stoning cars belonging to foreigners.

5. **SOMALIA**

In 1991, at least 65 people were killed in Mogadishu, Somalia, when security forces opened fire on the crowd during a soccer match after fans threw rocks at President Mohammed Siad Barre. At the time, Somalia was involved in a civil war that caused some 40,000 deaths and widespread famine.

6. **NEPAL**

At Katmandu, Nepal, in 1988, about 90 people died when soccer fans were trampled in a stampede to escape a hailstorm. The storm pelted a crowd of about 30,000 at a match at the National Stadium. Fans tried to get out of the stadium but found the gates locked.

7. NIGERIA

Nigeria and Ghana squared off on February 10, 1973, in World Cup qualifying in Lagos, Nigeria. The match ended in a riot. In the closing stages, Ghana scored a goal to take a 3–2 lead, but the crowd thought Ghana should have been called for offsides. Spectators started fires in the stands and hurled bottles, cans, and rocks onto the field. Officials called off the match, and troops were brought in to restore order. Nigeria was disqualified by the FIFA, and Ghana advanced to the next round of qualifying.

8. CAMEROON

Cameroon and the Congo met in a tense qualifying match for the World Cup on October 31, 1976, in Yauonde, Cameroon. The referee awarded a penalty kick to Cameroon and was attacked by the Congolese goalkeeper. A melee ensued, and Cameroon President Ahmadou Ahidjo, who had been watching the match on television, sent in paratroopers to quash the riot. The Congo won the match 2–1.

9. TURKEY

In Turkey, matches are often powder kegs because of ethnic and provincial division within the country. In September 1967, a contest between Kayseri Spor and Sivas Spor led to a riot in which 44 people were killed. A Kayseri player had been ordered off the field for continual foul play, but a shower of stones and verbal abuse from the home fans convinced the referee to reverse the decision. This incensed the thousands of visiting fans from Sivas, and fighting with pistols, knives, and bottles broke out. Civil War threatened to erupt between the provinces of Kayseri and Sivas, and the army was called in to patrol the border. In Sivas, businesses and automobiles belonging to people from Kayseri were vandalized.

10. **LIBERIA**

During a World Cup qualifier between Liberia and Chad in Monrovia, Liberia, on April 23, 2000, three fans died after being brutally beaten as a mob stormed the stadium. Many spectators waited eight hours in the hot sun to get into the stadium before storming the barbed-wire fences and over-powering police and soldiers. Some 50,000 to 60,000 jammed into the 33,000-seat stadium to watch a 0–0 draw.

Soccer-Style Kickers

One of soccer's greatest impacts on sports in the United States has been the transformation of the kicking game in U.S. football. The first soccer-style kicker, using the instep and approaching the ball from the side, appeared in pro football in 1964 and drove out all of the "straight ahead" kickers by 1981. The new approach rendered obsolete kickers—and nicknames—like Lou "The Toe" Groza. The success of the soccer-style kickers led to rules changes which moved the kickoff point from the 40-yard-line to the 30 and pushed the goalposts back from the front of the end zone to the rear.

1. PETE GOGOLAK

Pete Gogolak escaped one revolution to start another one. When he was 14, Pete and his family escaped Hungary and came to the United States after the Soviet Union crushed a revolt by the Hungarian people against the communist system. In 1964, after playing in college at Cornell, he became pro football's first soccer-style placekicker with the Buffalo Bills. Gogolak played for the Bills for two seasons and for the New York Giants from 1966 through 1974.

2. **CHARLIE GOGOLAK**

Pete's brother Charlie reached the NFL in 1966 after playing college ball at Princeton. Charlie lasted six seasons in the pros with the Washington Redskins (1966–68) and the Boston and New England Patriots (1970–72). On November 27, 1966, Washington coach Otto Graham sent Gogolak into the game with seven seconds remaining to kick a 29-yard field goal with the score 69–41 over the New York Giants. The kick was good, giving Washington an all-time record of 72 points scored in a game and breaking the old mark of 70 set by the 1950 Los Angeles Rams. The 113 combined points by the Redskins and Giants was also a record, and the placekickers for both teams were Gogolaks.

3. **GARO YEPREMIAN**

No one looked less like a pro football player than the balding, five-foot-eight-inch Garo Yepremian. His play matched his looks during Super Bowl VII on January 14, 1973. When a blocked field-goal attempt bounced back to Yepremian, he tried to throw the ball downfield, only to have it intercepted and returned for a touchdown by Washington's Mike Bass. Despite Yepremian's *faux pas,* his Miami Dolphins won 14–7. Born in Cyprus, Yepremian reached the NFL with the Detroit Lions in 1966 and played for 14 seasons.

4. **JAN STENERUD**

Utilizing skills he learned as a youngster on the soccer fields of his native Norway, Jan Stenerud became the first place kicker elected to the Pro Football Hall of Fame. He came to the United States on a skiing scholarship at Montana State University. Stenerud played for the Kansas City Chiefs

(1967–79), Green Bay Packers (1980–83), and Minnesota Vikings (1984–85). He kicked three field goals in Kansas City's 23–7 Super Bowl over Minnesota on January 11, 1970.

5. **CHRIS BAHR**

Chris Bahr's father, Warren, played on the 1950 U.S. World Cup team which upset England, and he later coached at Penn State. Chris was a soccer All-American at Penn State and doubled as a placekicker for the football team. In 1975, Bahr was the rookie of the year in the North American Soccer League while playing for the Philadelphia Atoms, but he gave up soccer for football. He played in the NFL with the Bengals, Raiders, and Chargers from 1976 through 1989. Chris's brother Matt lasted 17 season with six clubs in the NFL between 1979 and 1995.

6. **FRANK CORRAL**

Frank Corral grew up playing soccer in his native Mexico before his family moved to Riverside, California, when he was still a boy. In the 1979 NFC championship game, he scored each of the Los Angeles Rams' points on three field goals in a 9–0 victory over the Tampa Bay Buccaneers.

7. **CHESTER MARCOL**

Chester Marcol was born in Opole, Poland, and grew up in Michigan after his family emigrated to the United States. He kicked for the Green Bay Packers from 1972 through 1980. On September 7, 1980, he lined up for an overtime field-goal attempt against the Bears. The kick was blocked, but it bounced back to Marcol, who ran the ball into the end zone for a touchdown and a 12–6 victory.

8. JOHN SMITH

John Smith came to the United States from England and was involved in a bizarre incident in 1982 while playing for the Patriots against the Dolphins in a snowstorm in Foxboro, Massachusetts. With time running out and the score 0–0, a snowplow was needed to clear a spot for the ball prior to Smith's game-winning field-goal attempt. The kick was good for a 3–0 New England victory.

9. SEBASTIAN JANIKOWSKI

It's rare for a placekicker to be selected in the first round of the NFL draft, but Sebastian Janikowksi was chosen by the Oakland Raiders as the 17th overall pick in 2000. He grew up as a soccer player in Poland before starring on the gridiron at Florida State.

10. GARY ANDERSON

Born in Durban, South Africa, Gary Anderson became the NFL's all-time leading scorer in 2000. He has played for the Pittsburgh Steelers (1982–94), Philadelphia Eagles (1995–96), San Francisco 49ers (1997), and Minnesota Vikings (1998–present).

Suicides

Soccer, like other walks of life, hasn't been immune to those who sought to take their own life.

1. HUGHIE GALLACHER

Hughie Gallacher was one of England's top players during a career that lasted from 1921 through 1939. After his playing days ended, he became an alcoholic. In 1957, the day before he was to appear in court for assaulting his son, Gallacher walked in front of an express train.

2. CUBA

A fan began a tragic sequence of events by setting off a firecracker on December 11, 1976, during a World Cup qualifying match between Haiti and Cuba in Port-au-Prince, Haiti. Assuming the sound of the firecracker was gunfire, fans panicked and knocked down a soldier whose machine gun went off, killing two small children. Two more fans were trampled to death, and another died after jumping over a wall. The soldier made his way out of the stadium and turned the gun on himself.

3. **MATTHIAS SINDELAR**

Called "The Man of Paper" for his slender build, Matthias Sindelar was one of Austria's top players during the 1930s. He tried to keep his Jewish identity a secret during the Nazi regime. After a teammate told the authorities that Sindelar was Jewish, he gassed himself in his apartment.

4. **ABDON PORTE**

Abdon Porte was one of the stars of Uruguay's Nacional team during the 1910s, but he couldn't handle the inevitable decline all athletes suffer as they grow older. After he was taken out of the starting lineup in 1918, Porte walked into Nacional's stadium in the middle of the night and shot himself in the center of the field.

5. **HONDURAS**

Honduran fan Domingo Padilla was so upset over the "unjust" elimination of his team from the 1982 World Cup that he shot and killed himself.

6. **BANGLADESH**

Banu Begum was a 30-year-old woman from Bangladesh who faithfully followed the exploits of Cameroon's national team. After Cameroon was eliminated by England in the 1990 World Cup, she hung herself. Her suicide note read: "Now that Cameroon has left the World Cup, I am leaving this world."

7. **1950 WORLD CUP**

After Brazil unexpectedly lost the 1950 World Cup final to Uruguay, at least six people were so distraught that they leaped off the top of Maracana Stadium to their deaths.

8. **BRAZIL**

In Fortaleza, Brazil, 20-year-old Nilton Teixeira was so distressed over Brazil's loss to Italy in the 1982 World Cup that he put a revolver to his head and shot himself.

9. **RAMIRO CASTILLO**

One of Bolivia's most popular players, 31-year-old Ramiro Castillo committed suicide on October 18, 1997, a few months after his nine-year-old son died of liver disease. Castillo hanged himself inside his home. Only six days earlier, Castillo had played for the Bolivian national team in a World Cup qualifying match against Ecuador.

10. **JUSTIN FASHANU**

Justin Fashanu, a 36-year-old former British soccer star, was wanted in the United States on charges of sexually assaulting a teenage boy in Maryland. Fashanu was found dead in a garage in London on May 3, 1998. He had fled to England while police were searching for him and died by hanging himself. Fashanu had been set to coach a new minor-league team called the Maryland Mania in Columbia, Maryland, before taking his own life.

Bad Ideas

S ometimes things don't go as planned.

1. ITALY

Roma in Italy's Serie A gave two match officials gold Rolex watches worth $13,300 as Christmas presents in 1999 and less expensive watches to 37 other referees. The Italian soccer federation ordered the referees to return the "inappropriate" gifts. Roma officials defended the gesture as a "normal courtesy."

2. WHITMINSTER

The Whitminster club in England had its team picture printed in the newspaper with player Craig Hampton crouched on his haunches at the end of the first row with a smile and a bit more of his anatomy poking through his shorts than he intended. The overexposure somehow got past the embarrassed editors of the *Stroud News and Journal.*

3. **KEITH WISEMAN**

Keith Wiseman was forced to resign from the chairmanship of the English FA in January 1999, when he arranged an unauthorized $5.4-million payment to the Welsh FA. He had hoped the payment would secure backing for a position on FIFA's executive committee.

4. **MANCHESTER UNITED**

Manchester United coach Alex Ferguson blamed his team's 3−1 loss at Southampton on April 13, 1996, on the club's gray uniforms. Manchester United played the first half in gray and fell behind 3−0. Ferguson claimed that his players found it hard to pick each other out because of the color of the jerseys. The team switched to blue, white, and yellow shirts in the second half. The gray shirts had been worn mainly as a marketing gimmick and were sold in stores by the thousands. Manchester United officials said the team would never wear gray again and put the remainder of the shirts on sale at a discount.

5. **BRAZIL**

Brazilian soccer authorities ordered a national peace day on October 30, 1994, in response to outbreaks of fan violence. During the match between Palmeiras and reigning world-club champion Sao Paulo, six players were ejected after a mass brawl that had to be broken up by Brazilian riot police. Palmeiras star player Edmundo, sent off the field after a reckless tackle, traded insults with the Sao Paulo bench, slapped one player, punched another in the face, and aimed a kick toward the groin of a third. Edmundo said he was justified in committing general mayhem because a Sao Paulo player had insulted his mother.

6. **MEXICO**

Pique, the mascot of the 1986 World Cup, became the target of Mexican nationalists. The Speedy Gonzalez–like cartoon character of Pique had a pointed jalapeno pepper head which stuck up through a large yellow sombrero, a black handlebar mustache, red nose, and oversized soccer shoes. Many were outraged over Pique, believing the mascot perpetuated an unfair stereotype of the Mexican people. The mascot had been created by a Mexico City ad agency. One of Pique's creators didn't help matters when he declared the character was "a bit like the sleepy Indian taking a siesta against a tree."

7. **SOVIET UNION**

In 1975, leaders in the town of Cherkassy in the Soviet Union were so anxious to field a winning soccer team that city fathers recruited one from nearby Chernigov. The players were listed as employees in a local factory, though they never worked there. Instead, they were paid top salaries, billeted in a local hotel, and fed caviar. The plan fell apart when the players celebrated a victory by fighting and smashing furniture in a restaurant, causing injuries to other diners. The team ended up in jail. After the brawl, city leaders discharged the players.

8. **1982 WORLD CUP DRAW**

The 1982 World Cup draw was a debacle. Miniature soccer balls were placed in a giant drum to determine the matchups. The balls featuring the names of Peru and Chile were supposed to be left out so that they wouldn't be placed in the same group as South American rivals Argentina and Brazil, but somebody forgot to do so. As a result, the draw had to be restarted. This time, the soccer balls jammed in the drum, and one of them split in half.

9. NAPLES

During the 1988 European championships, almost the entire staff of San Gennaro Hospital in Naples walked out on patients to watch a match between Italy and Sweden in Naples. Thirty-nine hospital workers were arrested as a result of the walkout, and criminal charges were filed against 200 others.

10. ARGENTINA

Argentina was one of the heavy favorites to win the World Cup in 1958 in Sweden but failed to survive the first round. When the team returned to Buenos Aires, they were greeted by a hail of rotten vegetables and fruit. There were numerous reports in Argentine newspapers of "indiscipline and fraternization with Swedish girls."

Strange but True

Here is a collection of the unusual, abnormal, bizarre, odd, peculiar, extraordinary, and inexplicable.

1. GERMANY

In January 2000, two major German department-store chains yanked the distinctive yellow jerseys of Borussia Dortmund because scientists had discovered that the chemical tributylin in the shirts caused sterility in sea snails. Nike, which manufactured the shirts, released its own test results which indicated that the shirts were safe to wear.

2. ENGLAND

In 1976, a British family named their son after the entire Manchester United team. Graham Alex Jimmy Stewart Gerry Brian Martin Steve Sammy Stuart Lou Gordon David Tommy Matt Cross became an accomplished player in Walsall in Central England and once scored all eight goals for his school in an 8–0 victory. However, at the age of 15, he spurned a contract offer from Manchester United and signed instead with Leeds.

3. **GLOUCESTER CITY**

Amateur players from a club in Gloucester City, England, were hypnotized before a match in 1959 against Merthyr Tydfil and won 3–1. The hypnotist was 61-year-old Henry Blythe, who spoke to the players just before they took the field, telling them, "You will win. You will play as you never have before." Team manager Albert Lindon was unimpressed, saying that hypnotism was "a lot of hooey. Gloucester was simply the better team."

4. **NEW YORK CITY BLOOD BANKS**

In 1982, Dr. Johanna Pindrych, director of the Greater New York Blood Program, left for Europe in an attempt to locate additional sources of blood. Only a two-day supply remained in inventory. The blood bank imported much of its supply from West Germany, but production slowed to a trickle because citizens of the country were preoccupied with the World Cup. Officials in West Germany tried placing televisions in the bloodmobiles, but it didn't work. After giving blood, donors stayed to watch the matches and refused to leave.

5. **UNITED STATES**

National League baseball owners formed a soccer association called American League of Professional Football Clubs in 1894 to fill their ballparks during the fall. The teams were all in the East and had the same nicknames as the baseball teams—the Boston Beaneaters, the Baltimore Orioles, the Washington Senators, the Philadelphia Quakers, the Brooklyn Superbas, and the New York Giants. Play began on October 6, but the league folded in midseason following meager crowds and run-ins with immigration authorities over the importation of players from abroad.

6. ENGLAND

In 1967, David Exall, administrative manager of England's Birmingham City club, hired 12 miniskirted girls to parade around at halftime in an attempt to curb rowdyism. "If we can get the fans blowing wolf whistles at the girls," said Exall, "they may stop throwing bottles at the referee and the players."

7. SPAIN

Alfredo di Stefano, one of the world's great players during the 1950s while playing for Real Madrid, commissioned a half-ton sculpture of a marble soccer ball to be built in the backyard of his home in Madrid. Inscribed on the sculpture was a simple phrase: "Thanks, old girl."

8. DOGAN BABACAN

Dogan Babacan of Turkey was the referee for the opening match of the 1974 World Cup, played between West Germany and Chile in West Berlin. Babacan's wife and daughter in Istanbul went to a neighbor's house to watch the game on television, and while they were there, the Babacan family home was burglarized.

9. BERT TRAUTMANN

A former World War II German paratrooper named Bert Trautmann led Manchester City to England's FA Cup in 1956 at a time when memories of the war were still fresh. Trautmann had been taken prisoner during the war but remained in England rather than return home. He was in goal for Manchester City's 3–1 victory over Birmingham City in the final. Afterward, it was determined that Trautmann had suffered a broken neck during a collision early in the contest but still finished the match.

10. 1974 WORLD CUP

When West Germany met Poland in the 1974 World Cup semifinals in Frankfurt, West Germany, a downpour struck an hour before the match. The start was delayed for 30 minutes while the fire department pumped thousands of gallons of water from the field. Players had to scoop the ball out of the water instead of making ground passes. West Germany won 1–0 on a goal by Gerd Muller 14 minutes from the end.

A Kick in the Head

More of the unusual, abnormal, bizarre, odd, peculiar, extraordinary, and inexplicable.

1. WHITE ELEPHANTS

In 1978, Argentine treasury secretary Juan Aleman publicly criticized the $700 million the government was spending to host the World Cup, claiming the stadiums built for the matches would become "white elephants" after the tournament was over. In response, Aleman's Buenos Aires home was bombed, although no one was injured.

2. JOHANN CRUYFF

Holland's Johann Cruyff, the player of the year in Europe in 1971, 1973, and 1974, announced his retirement in 1978. He was persuaded to come out of retirement in 1979 to play for the Los Angeles Aztecs of the North American Soccer League. On May 23, 1979, in his first match with the Aztecs, Cruyff scored two goals in the first six minutes in a 3–0 victory over the Rochester Lancers. After netting 13 goals in 23 games, Cruyff was named NASL player of the year.

3. **A SCANDAL IN ITALY**

In 1980, Massimo Crociani, a fruit vendor, and restaurant owner Alvaro Trinca touched off a huge scandal when they filed lawsuits against 27 players from Italy's major teams. After losing large bets, the two men charged many of the country's top stars with accepting bribes to lose games, then changing their minds and winning. AC Milan, Italy's champion in 1979, was demoted to the second division by the Italian FA for its involvement in the betting scandal. Club president Felice Colombo was imprisoned for life for his role in rigging matches.

4. **A MARCH THROUGH THE MOUNTAINS**

Seven members of Afghanistan's national team defected to West Germany in 1980 and were granted political asylum. The group fled after refusing to play exhibition games in the Soviet Union. The players trekked through the mountains for three days to make their way to Pakistan, eluding Soviet guards and Afghan rebels. They stayed in a refugee camp for 12 days before obtaining forged passports for the flight from Karachi to Frankfurt.

5. **A RIOT IN CHINA**

On May 19, 1985, fans in China rioted after a 2–1 loss by the national team to Hong Kong in a World Cup qualifier at Peking Workers Stadium. There were 30 policemen injured, four of them seriously. A total of 127 were arrested, but 125 were released after receiving a "stern lecture." The light sentences were granted because Chinese leaders were concerned about negative press. The nation was intent on reassuring Hong Kong on its incorporation into China, scheduled for 1997.

The Chinese national soccer team was disbanded on May 31 for "bad sportsmanship" because they refused to shake hands with the Hong Kong team after the defeat and tried to drag an injured Hong Kong player off the field so the match could continue.

6. MURDER IN COLOMBIA

Dimayor, the Colombian soccer federation, canceled the remainder of the domestic soccer season after gunmen in Medilin shot and killed a referee on November 15, 1989, just hours after he officiated a match.

7. RECORD LOSSES

Heading into qualifying for the 2002 World Cup, the all-time record defeat was by Maldives at the hands of Iran in 1997. It was broken three times in a span of six months in 2000 and 2001. In its first ever World Cup qualifying match, Guam lost 19–0 to Iran on November 24, 2000.

8. GIL Y GIL

In 1969, a large convention hall was built in Spain's Guadarrama Mountains. During the grand opening, the floor collapsed, and 52 people were killed. The owner of the edifice was Jesus Gil y Gil, who spent 27 months in jail for constructing the hall with substandard materials, until pardoned by dictator Francisco Franco. Gil y Gil purchased the Spanish soccer club Atletico of Madrid in 1986 and fired 29 coaches in 10 years before winning the league championship in 1996. He was also elected mayor of the resort town of Marbella in 1991 but was jailed again six years later for misuse of public funds.

9. **BARGAIN BOOZE**

In 2001, the home field of the English professional club Witton Albion was renamed Bargain Booze Stadium after the discount liquor chain purchased the naming rights to the venue.

10. **JOHN THOMSON**

On September 5, 1931, Celtic's 23-year-old goalkeeper dove at the feet of Sam English of the Rangers and was kicked in the head. A member of Scotland's national team and one of the nation's most popular players, Thomson died five hours later from a fractured skull.

Bibliography

Books

Archer, Michael, editor. *The International Book of Soccer:* A&W Publishers, New York, 1977.

Galeano, Eduardo. *Soccer in Sun and Shadow:* Verso, London and New York, 1998.

Goldstein, Dan. *English Football: The Rough Guide:* The Rough Guides, London, 1999.

Goldstein, Dan, editor. *European Football: The Rough Guide:* The Rough Guides, London, 2000.

Hollander, Zander, editor. *The American Encyclopedia of Soccer:* Everest House Publishers, New York, 1980.

Murray, William J. *The World's Game: A History of Soccer:* University of Illinois Press, Champaign, 1996.

Radnedge, Keir. *The Complete Encyclopedia of Soccer:* Carlton, London, 2000.

Magazines

Soccer America, 1982–2001.

Newspapers

The New York Times, 1923–2001.

Index

About the Author

John Snyder has a Master's Degree in history from the University of Cincinnati and developed a passion for soccer when his two sons began playing the sport. He has authored eleven books on soccer, baseball, football, hockey, tennis, and travel. He lives in Cincinnati, Ohio.